MYTH AND REASON: A SYMPOSIUM

Myth and Reason
A SYMPOSIUM

Edited with an Introduction by
WALTER D. WETZELS

Published for the Department of Germanic Languages
of The University of Texas at Austin by the
University of Texas Press, Austin and London

Library of Congress Cataloging in Publication Data
Main entry under title:

Myth and reason.

"Lectures of Symposium 1971: myth and reason,
sponsored by the Department of Germanic Languages of
the University of Texas at Austin as delivered by their
authors April 12–14, 1971."
  Includes bibliographical references.
  1. German literature—Congresses. 2. Myth in
literature. 3. Reason. I. Wetzels, Walter D.,
1930, ed. II. Texas. University at Austin. Dept.
of Germanic Languages.
PT31.M9   830'.9   72–3096

Composition and printing by The University of Texas
  Printing Division, Austin
Binding by Universal Bookbindery, Inc., San Antonio

"Myth must be taken seriously as a cultural force but it must be taken seriously precisely in order that it may be gradually superseded in the interests of the advancement of truth and the growth of human intelligence."

David Bidney, in *Myth: A Symposium*
Ed. Thomas A. Sebeok
p. 14

CONTENTS

PREFACE

With two exceptions, this volume of essays represents the lectures of *Symposium 1971: Myth and Reason*, sponsored by the Department of Germanic Languages of The University of Texas at Austin as delivered by their authors April 12–14, 1971. Helmut Rehder's "Goethe and Leibniz: Myth in the Age of Reason," which could not be given at the time of the symposium, is included here as it was conceived in accordance with original plans for the event. A lecture by Oskar Seidlin, "The Lofty Game of Numbers: The Peeperkorn Episode in Thomas Mann's *Der Zauberberg*," which *was* given at the symposium, does not appear in this volume; it has recently been published in *PMLA* 86 (October, 1971): 924–939. With the consent of all participants, the round-table discussion which concluded the symposium has been edited to eliminate conversational redundancies while maintaining its natural tone.

An effort has been made to present the entire volume in English and yet preserve the authenticity of the original reference material. Unless otherwise stated, translations of German quotations and titles are those of the individual authors, with the original German appearing either in the footnotes or as part of the text with the English in brackets.

I would like to express my special gratitude to Mrs. Nancy Anne Zeller for her help in making the many arrangements for the symposium as well as in preparing this volume for publication.

WALTER D. WETZELS

Myth and Reason:
An Introduction

BY WALTER D. WETZELS

The University of Texas at Austin

While the terms *myth* and *reason*, particularly when expressed in German as *Mythos* and *Vernunft*, resound with profundity, their echoes in our minds are as distant as they are mighty. As concepts that have cast a long shadow in the tradition of the human experience, their contours are both suggestive and vague. Especially when presented interlocked by that inconspicuous conjunction "and," both concepts seem to generate a powerful field of attraction or repulsion which charges every fact and argument with an often explosive ambiguity. Whenever we feel ready to settle for the comfortable and seemingly fruitful symbiosis, the uneasy dialectic of the two notions keeps our minds restless and our emotions agitated. Too many historical memories and deep personal experiences seem to be conjured up by a constellation which, in the disguise of an intellectually tantalizing paradox, expresses a human calamity.

This attempt to introduce the problem and some of its rami-
fications first focuses on the present and then shifts to the past
in order to gain the perspective of history for the understanding of the possibly blind immediacy of our direct and often
unreflected experience. The description of *current* manifestations of myth and reason touches upon characteristics which
are more or less common to all societies of the Western world.
However, the *historical* context is a German context first, often
exclusively so. Generalizations and analogies, therefore, can
only be made with great care. While the limitations of this approach are obvious, there is at least one advantage to the provin-
cial setting: Germany's intellectual and political past provides
unusually rich and concrete evidence for the playful intermezzi
between myth and reason in the realm of literature, as well as
for powerful encounters between them in the lives of individuals and the history of the people. It is an enlightening and
often frightening case history of our problem.

If any age can be characterized as dominated by the forces of
rationality, it is *our* time. The prevailing spirit as well as its
technical implementations seems to demonstrate that rational,
analytic thinking and engineering have permeated our world to
such an extent that to speak of modern life is to do so in terms
of a rationalistic, technological civilization. Today, rational
analysis, its results for the present and its extrapolations into the
future, has invaded virtually every sphere of human endeavor
and is certainly at the core of almost every economic, social,
scientific, and technological undertaking. Most of the tools and
much of the spirit of rationality now play an increasingly important role, even in the discipline which traditionally has
claimed those human activities that seem to defy purely rational
modes and approaches: the humanities. To be "scientific" also in
the realm of human emotions, imaginations, and values has not
only become part of the occasionally rather desperate defense
mechanism against the "other" of the two cultures, but is also the

expressed or implied credo of much of the professional research and general thinking in the humanities, a field which used to be considered as harboring and also describing the nonrational faculties of man. All this is so widely known as to be almost a commonplace. But virtual truisms in expressing what is generally accepted tend to put a question to rest which ought to be kept alive. In the case of the obvious proliferation of rationality in our time it should be kept in mind that this includes the many and often strong doses of manipulated irrationality which are constantly being injected into our lives.

The rational spirit that so obviously governs and sustains our world originated, of course, in the natural sciences and is, in essence, the mathematical spirit which Descartes once conjured up (as did the sorcerer's apprentice in Goethe's ballade—who was then unable to remember the magic formula which would control the overwhelming activities of the spirit he had called into action). The suspicion that our present situation might be not at all dissimilar has been with us for some time, except that in Goethe's *Der Zauberlehrling* it is magic which gets out of hand, whereas few people would insist on carrying the analogy with the sorcerer's apprentice so far as to suggest that science might be our magic. In any case, whether one is alarmed, entertained, intrigued by a paradoxical analogy, or plainly frustrated by the experience of the phenomenon itself, there is a growing awareness, especially among the young, that ubiquitous, comprehensive organizing and engineering of our lives according to rational principles, instead of furthering the modest human ambition to lead a meaningful life, have on the contrary brought about a general atrophy of meaning. In order to escape from or to restructure a world in which rationality seemed to reign supreme, many took to time-honored and ever-present (perhaps even cleverly provided for) transrational pursuits of life. In the face of what appeared to be an existence void of real, personal significance, disillusioned with a way of life which distant ancestors and their self-appointed pallbearers had allegedly instilled with everlasting values, the young chose to reactivate an old human potential: the mythical consciousness of man. By so doing they reopened what seems to be the perennial arsenal for all counterforces to reason: myth, the emanations of which cover the spectrum from witchcraft and black magic through astrology and hallucinatory insights to various forms of mysticism.

Of course, to postulate the existence of a mythical consciousness as a special cast of the human mind, as a unique way of seeing and explaining the world with special features and categories of apprehension, is a debatable proposition. Here, it is employed merely as a working hypothesis, that is, its validity is determined only by its usefulness in finding characteristics which otherwise easily escape analysis, or—if they are encountered—are often dismissed as irrelevant, as irrational superstitions. The proposition of a mythical consciousness is useful because it not only allows for but invites the notion that the concepts in any given mythical system refer to some content. In other words, these concepts are charged with meaning besides forming a structure which in many ways may be similar to a rational frame of mind. If studying myth means limiting the investigation to the *formal* characteristics of mythical systems, it would seem to be difficult to disagree with Claude Lévi-Strauss who contends, of course, that there is, in fact, no evidence for any fundamental difference between a mythical and a rational mind. However, structural anthropology is paying a high price for its unquestionable achievements. Its resolute reductionism has led to the discovery of a basic logic in myths, a schema of binary oppositions in permutation and their mediation. At the same time, the fascination with the formal and in the end universal characteristics ignores the different modes and values of life which the elements of structure symbolize. This is done by rendering the entire question irrelevant to and outside of a genuinely scientific investigation of myth. Here the subject matter is defined by and in terms of a specific approach, the structural one. The procedure is methodologically proper, to be sure, but it is at the same time arbitrary with respect to the variety of manifestations of the phenomenon myth itself and the many angles of its refractions in the history of the human mind. As an introduction, therefore, a more general, less exclusive orientation seems to be advisable.

Both mythical and rational thinking aim at explaining, structuring, ordering the world. The intended structure is a closed universe, inhabitable for humans, oriented toward their needs and aspirations: a world meant for man. The sense of order and unity which myths give is one based on feeling and intuition which relates every thing and every being intimately to everything else. Moreover, it makes all creatures appear dependent on one another, thereby creating a feeling of the solidarity of all life. All members of the world are integrated into a whole that is an animated ecological system, instilled with moral values for man of what is right and wrong, once and for all. If man is not necessarily the center of this world, he has his definite and unchangeable place in it. Once he is initiated into the myths which provide for comprehensive orientation in his world, he has the finite set of answers to the finite set of questions that are, ever were, ever will be.

Rational intelligence does not originate from or promote a unity of feeling but, as Ernst Cassirer has described it, an intellectual unity.[1] The system in which it attempts to render a unified picture of the world is not an organic but a logical one; it is open at the beginning and open at the end by virtue of the constant testing of its earliest assumptions as well as its latest statements. The relations among all phenomena, their number

[1] See "Die Begriffsform im mythischen Denken," in Ernst Cassirer, *Wesen und Wirkung des Symbolbegriffs* (Darmstadt: Wissenschaftliche Buchgesellschaft, 1956), pp. 1–70.

and complexity being what they are, have to undergo a long process of analysis before any synthesis can be attempted. Analysis is a process of fragmentation rather than of unification, and any synthesis can only be a preliminary one soon to be questioned and dissolved. Thus the intellectual unity of the world is only achieved by an infinite number of infinitely small steps rather than in one act of faith. Rational truths have to be proven rather than accepted as a given tenet. Understanding becomes, in Galilei's terms, an "infinite task."

It is as a reaction to this never-ending journey of the intellect upon which Western man has embarked that we witness now the longing for the harbor. The questions seem endless, therefore the desperate embrace of whatever seems to offer answers. It is mythical truth which provides these answers and does so by revelation, at once and forever. Myths were before time, and therefore are beyond time, handing down their laws for all times and any conditions. With respect to our fellow men, myths unite us, where the intellect divides us; they carry us home into the family of all beings, where the intellect alienates us from them. But then, myths do not free man—they bind him. They spell out the laws which determine his life and lay out what will be his fate; they deny all real change, all human progress and emancipation, by emphasizing the universals in human nature and the permanence of a predetermined constellation with respect to the world and within the community of man.

It is not without irony that at a time when the young in the United States embrace the message of Hermann Hesse, when they seem to be longing for mystical internalization, most of their European and especially German counterparts are set on the very opposite course. Not only are the literary merits of the writer of *Siddhartha* and *Steppenwolf* considered dubious (and better not be mentioned at all in intellectual circles), but there is an obvious and general allergy against all forms of mythophilia. The young in Germany have decided to rid themselves of the famous and infamous legacy of *Innerlichkeit* and to throw themselves into the battle for the emancipation of reason and the liberalization of the individual within a better society for all, reviving—as they see it—the spirit of the eighteenth-century enlightenment and its feeble tradition in Germany. Such a revival of what was called the Age of Reason could not help but encounter the long and strong tradition of irrational undercurrents in Germany's past. In fact, it is likely that the rational fury which has seized many of Germany's young intellectuals today is the allergic reaction to the hideous climax of irrationality that presented itself as the new myth of the Third Reich, the vestiges of which they see still alive. It is then understandable that the scrutiny with which past and present are being reexamined is as often ruthless and biased as honest and revealing and is furthermore a necessary antidote against another outbreak of myth. It was during the second half of the eighteenth century that a cautious appreciation of myths, that is, of Greek and Germanic mythology, began, after and in part still while the Enlightenment had little but irony or scorn for the old tales about gods and heroes of the past. In Germany it was mainly J. G. Herder who tried to educate the sensibility of his sophisticated contemporaries, especially for archaic manifestations of human experience and inspiration. He saw mythical tales as a language of hieroglyphs which had to be deciphered rather than taken literally if they were to reveal their true meaning. To aid a perceptive interpretation of mythical figures, images, and events, Herder even presented an imaginative, persuasive genesis of particular motifs, which, for instance, in Greek mythology, were explained as originating from a people whose way of life and mode of thinking were strongly determined by the sea. Man who sails the oceans, who lives under vast skies in daily battle with totally strange, capricious, and powerful elements will project his fears and hopes into images that are taken from and reflect his concrete condition. Thus the fanciful tales become allegories of real human experience and of the quest to understand and to survive.

Herder's imaginative labors, demonstrating that on the basis of concrete geographical and psychological conditions (among others) myths did indeed make sense, were originally meant to make this long-ignored reservoir of symbols respectable again for reason. The generation of Romantics that began to make its influence felt on the intellectual and even scientific scene of Germany around 1800 made Herder's message its credo. For the Jena circle around the Schlegel brothers and Novalis the problem was no longer the respectability of myths, but their revival and infusion into the spirit of the time so as to create a new mythical age worthy of its ancient prototypes. Friedrich Schlegel's call for a "new mythology," which was to embrace the myths of the Orient, Spinoza's pantheism, and modern physics, was the articulation of a longing for a new unity of thinking and feeling, for a synthesis of all intuitive and rational knowledge. It was the expression of a *Heimweh* for the Golden Age, for the time when man felt at home in and at peace with a world which was the organic whole of all beings and a stable, intelligible universe for men. While this call, obscure and ambitious, was meant to be a provocatively conceived alternative, both in the terminology used and in the spirit invoked, to the determined rationalism of the Enlightenment, the envisioned spiritual universe still did provide for rational, even scientific, pursuits as integral parts of the mythical whole. It was not until the latter part of the nineteenth century that the term *Mythos* began to become the magic formula whose incantation would conjure up archaic "virtues" and elementary drives which were just as much beyond good and evil as they were beyond reason.[2] It was the worship of allegedly timeless

[2] For a description of the development of the term *myth* in German intellectual history see Theodore Ziolkowski, "Der Hunger nach dem Mythos: Zur seelischen Gastronomie der Deutschen in den Zwanziger

and strong impulses in man that led to the secret and overt af-
firmation of the grandiose, indeed sacred, simplicity and power
of these basic urges. A new morality was proclaimed whose sole
demand on man was that he satisfy these drives, that he realize
his nonrational potentials. Inevitably this new mythmaking had
to revive the Germanic and other heroic paradigms. Wagner
orchestrated his seductive yearnings for the rich and plain, the
barbaric and powerful Germanic past. Nietzsche's philosophy,
mobilized in the pose and tone of a biblical seer and in the
figure of Zarathustra, was beyond the plebeian notion that reasons should accompany new insights. Reason, tired of its own
sophistication, found itself strangely fascinated with the revelations of an archaic heroism, with the powerful certainty and
simplicity of its emotions and ideas. In the minds of the later
plagiarists and popularizers of Wagner and Nietzsche irrational
messianism reigned supreme. Around the turn of the century
this state of mind manifested itself in many forms of antirationalism, most conspicuously perhaps in the various obscure quests
for a new myth through the search for the mythical grail.[3] By
that time *Mythos* had indeed become a sacred word for many, a
promise for instant relief and wisdom and at the same time a
mandate to convert others, thus assembling an initiated elite
with a special blessing and therefore with a special privilege
over the uninitiated masses. The term then was to develop into
the code word which summoned all the forces that allegedly
determined the age, which contained the entire body of its basic
beliefs and evoked the final destiny of its movements. *Mythos*
thus had emancipated itself from mythology, and, in fact, from
history, to become the embodiment of the combined ideological

---

Jahren," in *Die sogenannten Zwanziger Jahre,* ed. Reinhold Grimm and
Jost Hermand (Berlin-Zurich: Verlag Gehlen, 1970), pp. 169–201.
    [3] See Jost Hermand, "Gralsmotive um die Jahrhundertwende," in *Von
Mainz nach Weimar: 1793–1919* (Stuttgart: Metzlersche Verlagsbuch-
handlung, 1969), pp. 269–297.

energies of the present. It is with this connotation that the term was used in Alfred Rosenberg's *Der Mythus des zwanzigsten Jahrhunderts.*

Playful indeed, compared with these developments, seems the tradition of the literary transfigurations of myths in Germany. When Goethe calls up the mythical figure of Helena in his *Faust,* he does so because she can serve as a symbol to represent through her legendary history man's idea of and fascination with beauty, the transitory, exhilarating, and destructive presence of the ideal in the real. Here myths are a poetic arsenal of symbols to be used as old prefigurations of new experiences. Through such symbols ideas can be depicted in such a way that the present becomes transparent and shows the contours of the mythical past as, conversely, the mythical past is preserved in the present. Thomas Mann likewise entertains and enlightens the reader in a deliberate and ironic artistic play with myth in many of his writings, but particularly in the tetralogy *Joseph and his Brothers.* The history of man's struggle to free himself of the mythical molds he was cast into while paying a pious-ironic tribute to those primordial forms is described in the stories of Joseph and his ancestors. It is the history of Western individualism, in its triumphs and pitfalls, the story about the ambiguity of becoming a self while rehearsing a mythical role. Such literary transfiguration of myth, that is, revivals in the modality of an "as-if," can give penetrating and memorable insights into the human condition. But to revive old or invent new myths as the driving force behind all reality, to reinstate the old gods and their worship into our times, so as to fashion our lives according to archaic forms, has proved at best to be nothing more than the nostalgic triviality of escapism from the labors of reason. At its worst it has led in recent German history to the barbaric messianism which, perverting an honorable tradition of testing the limits of rationality, succeeded in all but destroying what fragile tradition of reason and humanism there was. The original idea for this symposium was, therefore, from the very beginning influenced by this very German experience. Its purpose then was not only to keep the vexing question of rationality versus irrationality vital in an academic discussion, but also to help prevent reason's becoming dormant again or intoxicated with the enticements of myth.

Goethe and Leibniz: *Myth in the Age of Reason*

The University of Texas at Austin

Among Goethe's manuscripts that deal with the possible continuation and eventual completion of his *Faust* fragment there exists a paper of enigmatic content.[1] Undated and presumably written in great haste at the approximate midpoint of his poetic career—between 1797 and 1799—it contains several striking *aperçus* concerning the First Part, partially completed and printed, and the Second Part, barely plotted and still to be executed. Of particular interest is a cryptic formula distinguishing the function of the two parts and their interpretation. Whereas the First Part is summarized as portraying "Lebens Genuß der Person von außen ges(ehen)" [enjoyment of life, in terms of the person, seen from without], various topics projected are envisioned for the Second Part, but in

---

[1] Johann Wolfgang von Goethe, *Faust,* "Paralipomenon 1," *Goethes Werke* (Weimar: H. Böhlau, 1887–1912), Part 1, vol. XIV, p. 287.

an inverted perspective, in that they are to express "Thaten Genuß nach außen" [enjoyment of action, externalized] and ultimately, "Schöpfungs Genuß von innen" [creative enjoyment from within]. Whatever the meaning of these terms, their terse juxtaposition seems to point to a specific poetic program even though it poses perceptual difficulties of utter complexity.

Dwelling on this problem means intensifying it. For example, the reader wonders whether the level of observation which assigns the enjoyment of life ("Lebens Genuß") to the person, the empirical individual, still obtains on the level of "Thaten Genuß" and "Schöpfungs Genuß," since the latter, presumably, transcend that level. It may be asked whether the latter two forms of "enjoyment" may not exceed the sphere of comprehensibility altogether, since the "person" no longer figures as reference point and the subject of enjoyment may be conceived as transcendental and beyond the sphere of empirical consciousness. Perhaps the metaphoric or symbolic use of the terms "from without" and "from within" is but a rhetorical device to distinguish the unessential from the essential—a device which is as old as poetry itself, vaguely intimating a fondness for absolutes and permanence in man's endeavor to orient himself in space and time. Ultimately, these endeavors coalesce in the extreme positions of science and mysticism and the infinite variety of attitudes between them which scorn or tolerate one another, depending on the latitude of imagination—or on the degree of certitude of insight into the nature of space and time. The brevity of the "Schema" for *Faust*, undertaken to compress the incommensurable into *one* formula, seemingly comprehensible and communicable, reflects the underlying human situation: after the first step, made with all the assurance and sweep and conviction of the poetic vision—"Ideales Streben nach Einwircken und Einfühlen in die ganze Natur. Erscheinung des Geists als Welt und Thaten Genius" [Ideal endeavor to gain intimate potency and communion with all of nature. Apparition of the (Earth) Spirit as genius of world and vitality]—the poet sees himself halted by the chill of reflection, the danger of premature generalization. He proposes to intensify the disparity between *Form* [configuration] and *Gehalt* [content] which, in the end, would lead to a fruitless argumentation about "emptiness" and "formlessness." More fruitful, it appears to him, would be the attempt to resolve the contradictions between "cold" and "warm" scientific effort, and, having regained his assurance in a manner of thinking suggesting an age-old belief in mysterious correspondences between macrocosm and microcosm, he develops his theory, his credo "vom Wesen der Dinge" [on the nature of things], sometimes halting to counter some reservations, sometimes adding a new perspective, but always committed to his conviction— the relevance of the view "from within."

As a denizen of the age of reason Goethe shared its faith in both the analytic and the integrative powers of reason. But he kept aloof from the metaphysical disputes of the philosophers who were arguing the *origins* of the notions of space and time. Whether their approach was empirical or speculative, their result was an abstraction equally inapplicable to his own mode of observing and experimenting with individual phenomena of physical or biological nature. Even Kant's demonstration of the subjective, or formal, nature of space and time turned out to be a prescriptive rather than a descriptive concept; it was more concerned with the conditions of mind and knowledge than with the conditions of nature and life when he declared time to be "the inner sense."

Whatever this "inner sense" may have meant to Kant in the analysis of the cognitive process, more significant was the concept of the *boundary* of empirical experience which characterized his stand in matters of nature. By defining and reinforcing the scope and function of scientific investigation, he liquidated the claims of mysticism and the lure of speculation. And yet, the very concept of reason, which had led him to assume the limitation of knowledge, prompted a corresponding expansion of thinking brought on by the notion of totality—"das Ganze." Kant never denied the idea or even the image of totality; while he ruled it out as an object of knowledge and cognition, he admitted it as a piloting and propelling force behind all intellectual endeavor, whether in the form of organic *unity* in nature and art, in the form of *continuity* in nature and history, or in the form of an absolute *postulate* in ethics and religion.

There is an element of painful ambiguousness in the notion of *totality*. While a "whole" can be observed and experienced in many different ways—a sonnet, a fruit, a flower, a crystal, a city, an age, any living organism—its conditions defy definition. It governs motion and growth while it is clearly beyond them. As a function it figures in calculus; in itself it appears incalculable. Accordingly, Kant ascribed to the notion of totality the function of a "regulative principle" which, applied to objective reality, "Gegebenheit," presupposes a synthesis "von außen," no matter how infinitesimal the steps or stages or how gigantic the leap of that approach.

By contrast, Goethe's postulate to view the processes of nature and poetry "from within" appears so consistent as principle and at the same time so diversified in application that it seems to derive from more than mere feeling and intuition. Feeling is formless and attached to the present; intuition is timeless and bestows an element of form; and since *form* unavoidably suggests an external, measurable quality, even the concept of *innere Form* [inward form], which Goethe employed in one of his early critical essays, cannot escape the charge of a compromise. Still, the manner in which he sought to apprehend the whole, aware of the dangers of abstraction and the risks of premature generalization, indicates a perspective in which the general and the unique are merged and the present is suspended in the flow of change. The evolving paradox, "Geprägte Form, die lebend sich entwickelt" [the form impressed which, living, grows and grows], culminates in a concept of reason that has gone far beyond the systematizing and timid practices of rationalism and, in absorbing feeling and intuition, has arrived at a point from which *Sinn* and *Kraft*—meaning and potency, mind and life—are taken to be but different aspects of the same principle. This idea of the whole inspired his poetic imagery; it dictated the structure of many of his plays, the composition of his novels, the discursive terminology of many of his critical essays. As a methodological proposition it guided his morphological studies and the "inner structure" of his *Faust*.

Tracing the genesis and evolution of Goethe's approach "from within" may be an attractive but intractable operation. It is plainly suggested in the delightful little parable of the stained church windows—"Gedichte sind gemalte Fensterscheiben" [Poems are like painted windowpanes]—which appear gloomy and drab when seen from the marketplace and turn into a miraculous play of color and light and meaning to the "children of God" who enter the chapel. Many of Goethe's early ballads, his "Märchen," even his discursive poems dealing with the metamorphosis of plants and animals, revolve around the hypothetical quest to view the elements "from within." The almost ubiquitous symbolism of the casket, of *schließen* [lock] and *Schlüssel* [key], seems to be based on similar assumptions. Often the possession of the center—the "hut"—is viewed as a token of grace, whereas the opposite drive, the desire to break out from the center of equilibrium, appears as a sign of *Verworfenheit*, rejection and fall from Divine Grace. The hapless wanderer, gurgling his "semi-nonsense" in the poem "Wanderers Sturmlied" [Wanderer's Storm Song] is desperately searching for an innermost point of security, "Innre Wärme/Seelenwärme/Mittelpunkt!" [inward warmth/spirit-warmth/central point], whereas the Faust of the First Part is impatiently seeking to break out from his confines "wo selbst das liebe Himmels-

licht trüb durch gemalte Scheiben bricht" [where even the
lovely light of heaven breaks wanly through the painted panes].
Such imagery, operating *directly* with dimensions of space and
locale, creates an atmosphere of enormously vibrant symbolism.
It expresses the search for meaning in a *direct* analogy to
fundamental physical phenomena—centripetal and centrifugal
motion.

Of particular significance is the beginning, and even the entire play of the *Egmont* tragedy. While all efforts to interpret
this play in the tradition of a historical, social, or political drama
meet with difficulties because they view the play "from without," as a conflict between particular and therefore incidental
factions, the play appears to be most carefully designed and
structured "from within," in a latent pattern of progressive
spiritualization, as the tragedy of a people delivered by the
sacrificial death of their "savior." To prepare for this image of a
"Volk," of whom Egmont is but an ideal though charismatic ex-
ponent, Goethe employs the three stages of the first act in an
increasing manner of intensification, symbolizing the physical,
intellectual, and spiritual aspects of the "people." Penetrating,
as it were, from the periphery to the center, "von außen nach
innen," through three concentric spheres of existence and activity, the action passes from the amorphous organism of a
nation at leisure and play through the brain cell of legal gov-
ernment to the inner sanctum of soul, the house of his beloved,
from which Egmont draws the strength of his mission. On each
of these three stages of materialization the undefinable power of
attraction—sympathy, affection, love—finds its appropriate, intensified mode of expression. Much of the lyrical quality for
which the play is known rests on the oscillating effect of this
inner structure: its hazy emotionalism, the growing opaqueness
of intuition, the haunting effect of tonal and musical structure,
the hidden allusions to the Christ figure, the striking transformation of a clandestine amour, significantly named "Klare,"

into an anima figure assuming the role of the "whole" people. More significant even is the intensity with which Goethe, in the light of later retrospect, associated the Egmont play with the phenomenon of the "daemonic," that very element of myth-making inwardness. On the borderline between religious and Gnostic consciousness, it manifests itself in ultimate contradictions. What distinguishes the Egmont plot is the kind of dramatic motivation it employs. It is neither fully psychological because it is permeated with allegories, nor is it entirely mystical because it makes use of quite realistic political and economic considerations. Both the hero and his sinister antagonist (Alba) operate in peculiarly double dimensions, as historical individuals and as symbolic principles. Egmont grows like a plant in un-knowing abundance from day to day. Alba comes to be the principle that impedes that growth. Between them there unfolds that enormously fascinating sphere of life, of growth and decline, of action and change, that sometimes appears calculable, more often unpredictable—that sphere to which Goethe later variously applied the term "das Werdende" [that which is coming to be] or the term "das Dämonische" [the daemonic], depending on the beneficial or detrimental aspect he had in mind. In his autobiographical account he had this to say: "Although the daemonic element can manifest itself in every corporeal and incorporeal domain, and is even expressed most remarkably among animals, it does have a most marvellous connection with human beings; and it constitutes a power which, though not opposing the moral order of the world, does cut across that order, whence one might regard the moral order as the warp and the other as the woof" [translated by Christopher Middleton].[2]

---

[2] "Obgleich jenes Dämonische sich in allem Körperlichen und Unkörperlichen manifestieren kann, ja bei den Tieren sich aufs merkwürdigste ausspricht, so steht es vorzüglich mit dem Menschen im wunderbarsten Zusammenhang und bildet eine der moralischen Weltordnung wo nicht

The allusion to the concept of the loom and the activity of weaving calls to mind a twofold frame of reference. On the one hand, it suggests the daemonic apparition of the Earth Spirit in one of the oldest scenes of *Faust*, where the entirety of the cosmos is envisaged under the image of the "loom of time"; on the other, it points to one of the most archaic occupations of man that figure in the anthropological analysis of myth, weaving—the weaving of the veil that conceals nature, or the weaving of any kind of texture or garment that enshrouds human nakedness or the radiance of the deity. Such allusions single out the *Faust* poem as the medium in which a mythical element coalesces into striking imagery—the image of the Earth Spirit in the First Part and the image of Helena in the Second —both visions sufficient to demonstrate the progressive internalization of viewpoint aiming at the visualization of totality, *das Ganze*. As Goethe completed the First Part, he altered the original manuscript version, which had ended with Margaret's voice, plaintively fading into darkness, to read "Stimme (von innen) verhallend" [voice (from within) fading away], thereby unnoticeably making the dungeon assume enormous symbolic dimensions. And when, in the visionary scene at the close of the entire play, the immortal part of Faust's entelechy is carried upward and on by the souls of unborn infants, the latter acquire the ability to behold reality from Pater Seraphicus who "takes them within himself" so that they see the nature of things through *his* eyes and, accordingly, from within.

Such formulations, of course, are no more than expressions of

---

entgegengesetzte, doch sie durchkreuzende Macht, so daß man die eine für den Zettel, die andere für den Einschlag könnte gelten lassen" (Johann Wolfgang von Goethe, "Dichtung und Wahrheit," *Gedenkausgabe der Werke, Briefe und Gespräche*, ed. Ernst Beutler [Zurich: Artemis, 1948–1954], X, 841). Further references to this edition are cited as Goethe, vol. title, Artemis (vol. no., page no.).

poetic *intentions*, bubbles thrown up from a boiling imagination, which in no way betray the manner in which the poetic substantialization of *inwardness* is to be achieved. It is at this point that the concept of *myth* offers some degree of methodological usefulness that is doubly rewarding. For it contains, on the one hand, an almost demonstrable manifestation of *boundary* as it derived from Kant's postulate of reason as the power of synthesis at the limits of experience; and it fulfills, on the other, the function of the heuristic principle of *totality* which Goethe assigned to the workings of poetic imagination, operating sometimes in conjunction with, sometimes in opposition to, the analytic method of scientific inquiry.

Myth is the image of timelessness beyond the limits of memory. To visualize the nature of myth, an analogy from spatial observation may be helpful. Just as a mountain range at the horizon appears as a continuous chain of peaks, although these peaks may be of different spatial distance and depth, myth appears as a continuous chain of primordial events—tales of cosmological or anthropological action—equally beyond the grasp of memory and historical consciousness. Cast, as it were, on a screen of infinite remoteness and no longer subject to the laws of perspective, myth takes on the appearance of transcendence without being transcendent. Concerning the nature of myth, Nietzsche made an unobtrusive though most provocative observation when he wrote, in his *Birth of the Tragedy*, "Only a horizon surrounded by myths completes the totality of a whole culture."[3] The connection drawn by Nietzsche between the concepts of myth and horizon is striking: both refer to objectives equally inaccessible to detailed analytic scrutiny. Doubtless Nietzsche was prompted to this observation by the ideas of Friedrich Schlegel and some of his contemporaries who

---

[3] "Erst ein mit Mythen umstellter Horizont schließt eine ganze Kulturbewegung zur Einheit ab" (Friedrich Nietzsche, *Werke in drei Bänden,* ed. Karl Schlechta [Munich: Hanser, 1960], I, 125).

deplored the apparent lack of a unifying intellectual principle of their time and called for the formulation of a new "mythology" characteristic of their own age. Friedrich Schlegel saw tokens of such a unifying, all-encompassing tendency in various intellectual movements of the times—for example, the "great phenomenon" of philosophical idealism, the emergence of a "new physics," the revival of Spinozistic pantheism, the spirited alternation between enthusiasm and irony.[4] Obviously both Nietzsche and Schlegel were occupied with the problem of the *physiognomy of an age*—the question whether the diversity and indeed the chaos of movements and beliefs in any given age may lend themselves to the discovery of an underlying intellectually structural pattern symbolizing totality, *das Ganze*. For centuries humanists and critics of culture have sought to diagnose and interpret the "intellectual situation" of their own present. There are many reasons to justify, and as many reasons to doubt, the wisdom of such an enterprise. Goethe, for example, cautioned that within a given epoch there is no one vantage point from which a universally valid view might be possible.[5] Schlegel, on the other hand, conceded that in every individual writer the "spirit of the age" assumes a different configuration, even though all of them seem to be united in a community of style and *Weltanschauung*. In both instances the humanistic position is based on man's relation to his horizon, that apparent limit of our vision where the multitude of things observed merges into an *image of totality*, reliable enough to function as a basis for orientation and navigation. Since the horizon is only virtually the same for all human beings and depends on the relative eye-level altitude of the individual observer, the world does look different if a person's horizontal plane is one foot above the ground, or six feet, or forty thousand

---

[4] Friedrich Schlegel, "Rede über die Mythologie," in *Kritische Schriften*, ed. Wolfdietrich Rasch (Munich: Hanser, 1956), pp. 306–317.

[5] Goethe, *Maximen und Reflexionen*, Artemis, IX, 629.

feet, or whether, as Leibniz postulated, he contemplates things "from the vantage point of the stars," in order to approximate his insight and judgment to that of Providence.[6] As a person progresses, his horizon moves with him, equally distant, that sharp line of demarcation where, metaphorically speaking, the future enters his vision as the past recedes behind him. No explorer has ever reached his horizon. He may rise until the curvature of the earth becomes visible and begins to shrink away underneath. Eventually Canopus or some other star in outer space takes on the function of reference point on the horizon. But no explorer has ever reached his horizon.

The same restriction may be applied to the realm of myth. As the all-encompassing image of "life" within a culture, it seems to recede from our grasp into that horizon of pastness which cannot be reached by any kind of rational analysis or reconstruction. According to Schlegel's definition, it is the nature of myth that "it sets aside the process and the laws of rationally thinking reason"—"der vernünftig denkenden Vernunft." But while it defies the abstractions of dialectical thinking, it appears to be operative under the laws of reality and life itself, the law of *polarity*, for example, or the laws of *unity* and *continuity*, which admit an element of infiniteness even within the scope of a spatially or temporally finite world. For infinity is open-ended in two directions: outwardly in the infinity of the universe, and inwardly in the infinity of the individual, the two opposites to which human inquiry, scientific or mystical, has been consistently devoted in a long tradition of *philosophia perennis*, that twilight zone between experiment and hypothesis where the mind gropes for analogies when the data are missing.

This feature of anonymity and universality seems to distinguish the realm of myth from any particular "philosophy," "world

[6] Gottfried Wilhelm Leibniz, "Von dem Verhängnisse," in Werner Burkhard, *Schriftwerke deutscher Sprache* (Aarau: Sauerländer, 1946), II², 3–7.

view," or creed—each of which, however archaic, still carries a seal of historical origin in some fashion or other. For the same reason it eludes the grasp of disparate intellectual disciplines. Myth is abundant in images into which man has projected his own existential situation; but myth is not the prerogative of artistic or aesthetic analysis alone. It resembles religion, but it resists the theological approach. It appears irrational, but it displays a peculiar rationality of its own. Reflecting primitive human habits, it may glow with flashes of utter sophistication. Ostensibly a repository of dreams and fears and desires and other phenomena of the collective unconscious, myth invites attention to the genesis of symbolic forms in the intimacy of the individual experience.

When Goethe posed the problem of poetic creativity from within ("innere Schöpfungskraft"), he was approaching the problem of myth from the vantage point of the age of reason. Necessarily he employed the terminology of that age even though inspired by protest. Thus it may be considered a handicap—or even an advantage—that the philosophical lingo of the German Enlightenment distinguished between two modes of thinking or reasoning, depending on the demonstrability of an object of cognition. To Goethe, as to many others, *Vernunft* enjoyed a higher degree of authenticity than *Verstand*, precisely because *Vernunft* [reason] carried with it a claim to universality of insight which was lacking in the faculty of *Verstand* [understanding]. With this distinction in mind, Goethe could write: "Die Vernunft ist auf das Werdende, der Verstand ist auf das Gewordene angewiesen" [*Vernunft* bears on that which is coming to be; *Verstand* bears on that which has become].[7] However indebted Goethe may have been to the rationalistic distinction between upper and lower faculties of the mind, what seems more significant at this point is the fact that he attributes an on-

---

[7] Goethe, *Maximen und Reflexionen*, Artemis, IX: 571.

tological priority to *das Werdende* over *das Gewordene,* and that in terms of poetic language *das Werdende* emphasizes an aspect of present and activity, whereas in *das Gewordene* these features have given way to inactivity and pastness. Although these terms reflect no more than the rationalistic distinction between the *natura naturans* and the *natura naturata* of pantheism, as a poetic device, the polarity of *das Werdende* over against *das Gewordene* allows an immense range of applicability: it stands for more than the relatively simple and rigid duality of "living" and "dead," of creation versus destruction, even of good and evil. We sense that in this poetic device something is being visualized which is of the utmost importance—the capturing of existence in the medium of words without the interference of chilling cerebration. Thus, for an instant, a light is shed on the meaning of *Mythos*—the authenticity of the spoken "word," in contrast to *Logos,* the "word" as the result of ratiocination and interpretation. *Das Gewordene* is accessible to analysis and comparison, *das Werdende* is not. As soon as the poet reaches for a *formula of totality,* an image of inwardness appears: "umfass' euch mit der Liebe holden Schranken" [wall you around with love, serene, secure].[8] *Logos* takes over to make this image communicable: "befestiget mit dauernden Gedanken" [fix ye it firm in thoughts that must endure (MacNeice, p. 16)]. We do not *know* what *das Werdende* is, as an object of cognition, although at the beginning and at the end of the play it looms large in the image of the encompassing. This is not stated as a guiding idea eventually to be illustrated in the Faust play in an allegorical fashion—a thought which Goethe rejected. Rather it is suggested, like a passing, marginal remark, to be kept in mind as the play unfolds. But as it unfolds we sense that *das Werdende* refers to an incommensurable totality,

---

[8] Louis MacNeice, trans., Goethe's *Faust,* Parts I and II (London: Faber & Faber, 1951, p. 16). Further references to this work will be listed parenthetically as MacNeice, with page no.

viewed from within, remaining beyond reach, like the horizon.

The manner in which the problem of *das Werdende* is poetically dealt with by Goethe, particularly in the prologue and in
the last scene of *Faust*, deserves some scrutiny. As a concept, it
remains vague enough to discourage externalization. As a symbol, it passes through several levels of rational endeavor, all of
them inadequate—"alles Vergängliche, das Unzulängliche, das
Unbeschreibliche" [all that is past of us, all that was lost in us,
all indescribables (MacNeice, p. 303)] before it culminates in
an *act* of life. Thus *das Werdende* is conceived as a form of
energy or force, peculiarly unencumbered by matter or mind,
alternately assuming a modus of contraction and expansion—
Einschränkung und Ausbreitung—seemingly natural drives that
guide the conception and composition of Goethe's works from
his early Storm and Stress to his old age. Consequently, our
mode of formulating Goethe's concept of *das Werdende* through
a polarity of process and form, or of dynamics and configuration, results in an impasse, because it inevitably substitutes that
which has become for that which is coming to be. In other
words, the portrayal of *physical* phenomena and their *metaphysical* explanation go hand in hand; and even though Goethe
denied the latter and insisted that he observed the operation of
ideas in nature, his faith in *das Werdende* remains a metaphysical postulate. If it were possible to take this poetic device seriously and interpret Goethe's views on *das Werdende* as an
attempt to envision the internal structure of energy—just as
seventeenth- and eighteenth-century thinkers attempted to envision the internal structure of matter and mind—the result
might have been *Epos*, the authentic verbal account of the nature of things, in the manner of Parmenides or Empedocles or
Lucretius' *De natura rerum*. Again we notice the unavoidable
shrinking of the intended totality before the claim of logical
commensurability. Perhaps it was incidental that, when Goethe
was pondering the completion of *Faust*, he was also considering

the possibility of an epic on nature. In fact, something of this sort had existed in Germany for nearly a century and a half, in the *Monadology* of Gottfried Wilhelm Leibniz, if we give credence to Herder, the master of hyperbole, who praised Leibniz the philosopher as the "großen Erfinder des Monadenpoems" [the great composer of the poem on monads].[9]

Leibniz's *Monadology*—no poem, but rather an abstract—is indeed an ingenuous combination of reason and imagination. In ninety succinct axioms it contains his doctrine of *substance*, that elusive objective of age-old philosophical thinking, that mysterious concept of Being which is thought to "underlie" all perceivable conditions, appearances, and effects. The image of what rests "at the bottom of things" has varied. While Spinoza conceived of it as an undifferentiated, infinite "One and All," Leibniz understood it to be an infinite variety of individual beings, the "monads," distinguished by their uniqueness and unrepeatability. It is not easy to discern the roots of divergence between Spinoza and Leibniz. Perhaps the one was guided by the notion of extension, the infiniteness of space, whereas the other was impressed with the intensity of thinking and occupied with the infinity of time. While both regarded substance under the aspect of *unity* and *continuity*, Spinoza contemplated its realization in the present—the arrested moment, if you will—while Leibniz emphasized the pregnance of the present with the future. "Le présent est gros de l'avenir," is one of his favorite maxims. Thus Spinoza's view of "substance" appears to culminate in the idea of virtual, static totality, whereas Leibniz's "substance" is constituted and characterized by activity, change, and dynamics. Needless to emphasize that these distinctions do not apply to an analysis of reality but rather to a philosophical world view which insists on introducing the auxiliary notion of substance as an intermediary construct between the observer

[9] Johann Gottfried von Herder, *Herders Sämtliche Werke*, ed. Bernhard Suphan (Berlin: Weidmann, 1877–1913), VIII, 178.

and the observed. But it *does* seem significant that the idea of totality, so akin to mythical thinking, finds its equivalent in the mythical concept of substance that forms the starting point of Leibniz's inquiry. In the terminology of the eighteenth century one might call his venture a *Gemälde* [panorama] of totality such as was undertaken a century later by Alexander von Humboldt in his *Kosmos* or by Hegel in his *Phänomenologie des Geistes* [Phenomenology of Mind]. But what the later thinkers expanded into comprehensive systems of description and analytic demonstration, Leibniz attempted to come by in the brevity of one grasp, in the grand gesture of one sweep. He does not offer, as other thinkers have done, a searching confession of self or a solemn vision of things to come. He restricts himself to a sober descriptive analysis, even though the object of his analysis is "das Unbeschreibliche." Thus there is an element of irony in Leibniz's treatise, but it is an irony of subject matter rather than of sentiment. Like Faust, he seeks to apprehend the condition and structure of life—and finds himself reduced to notions and analogies. He believes in vitality and becomes ensnared in theories of vitalism. A protagonist of consciousness, he becomes the discoverer of the subconscious, even though it was left to later ages to articulate that sphere. Like Hegel's *Phenomenology*, a philosophical enterprise of astonishing scope, the *Monadology* owed its purpose to the "Anstrengung des Begriffs" [the effort of comprehension] as the sine qua non of genuine philosophical activity; and, like Hegel's work, it became the initiator of an anemic school of formalistic rationalism.

As a hypothesis, the *Monadology* probes into the meaning of unity and diversity, of the general and the unique, of being and change. It deals with the problem of the beginning and the end of existence, the meaning of first and final causes, eternal verities and verities of fact. It plays, as a musician "plays," with the relation between matter and mind, body and soul, activity and receptivity, confusion and clarity. We read about inward principles and their outward realization; we sense the priority of organic over mechanistic causality, the superiority of metamorphosis over rigid form. If anywhere in the brief document there is room for subjective leanings and faith, it is in the assumption of a possible ultimate order and harmony, established by Divine Grace; or it is in the fundamental aversion toward the notion of empty space. That is why Leibniz seems to prefer to speak about monads and entelechies rather than about atoms. For the monads, described as perennially active in motion and relation, appear to him as the smallest imaginable bearers of motion, themselves enacting and reflecting it. Herder was deeply impressed with Leibniz's manner of interpreting motion as a manifestation of *eines inneren Zustandes* [an inner condition] which he called *Vorstellung* [idea]—leaving it undecided whether he was speaking as a theologian or as the popularizer of a philosophy of life.

The question is whether the theme of *das Werdende*, as it monopolized Goethe's thinking, owes its origin to the notion of monads, and to Leibniz's *Monadology* in particular. We know that Goethe placed an enormous significance on the human requisite of action, activity: "Des echten Mannes wahre Feier ist die Tat" [The true festivity of man is deed]. This is but an intensified form of the fundamental condition of all existence—activity and change. "Dieweil ich bin, muß ich auch tätig sein" ["While I exist I must show energy" (MacNeice, p. 199)], Homunculus remarks in a sort of monadological self-definition. The puzzling formula of "Thaten Genuß nach außen" which Goethe included in his laconic plan of 1797 for the completion of *Faust* leaves us without any immediate and applicable clues. It may, or may not, refer to any particular or heroic "deed" of a dramatic character in the Second Part, say, Euphorion. If it does, it only demonstrates the operation of a fundamental inner principle of effectiveness, accountable for the emergence of form and metamorphosis. While "Thaten Genuß" and "Schöpfungsgenuß" clearly transcend the level of the "person," they can be envisioned as potential states of the monads, seen "from within."

Contemplation on monads or entelechies in Goethe's writings leads only to thin evidence of an "influence" of Leibniz. Pythagoreans and Giordano Bruno played with similar concepts, too. The seriousness, however, with which Goethe, in his *Morphological Notebooks* (1822), speaks about "life, as the rotating movement of the monad around itself,"[10] and the genuine respect with which he compared Wieland to a monad in the Leibnizian sense[11] leave little doubt that he was familiar with Leibniz's manner of interpreting energy. Probing into the origins of Goethe's thought reveals an admirable effort. But when we find that many individual thinkers—Heraclitus, Plotinus, Paracelsus, Giordano Bruno, Boehme, Swedenborg, Hippocrates, the Orphics, the Cabbalistic *Aurea Catena Homeri*, and, more recently, the abstruse occultism of "hermetic philosophy"—are given the responsibility for having engendered and shaped Goethe's thought, we hesitate to add Leibniz to this intellectual horizon as a further factor of differentiation and fragmentation. Leibniz himself—the universal mind and supreme eclectic—had this to say about his own philosophical credo:

This system shows that if you go to the bottom of things you will discover more reason [Vernunft] in most of the philosophical schools than you had previously anticipated. The meager substantial reality taught by the Sceptics; the reduction of all things to harmonies and numbers taught by the Platonists; the all-embracing fundamental One-ness of Parmenides and Plotinus which still differs from Spinozism and the Stoics; the vitalism of Cabbalistic and Hermetic philosophers who assume sensation everywhere; the forms and entelechies of Aristotle and the Scholastics which do not exclude the

---

[10] *"Das Höchste, was wir von Gott und der Natur erhalten haben, ist das Leben, die rotierende Bewegung der Monas um sich selbst . . ."* Goethe, *Maximen und Reflexionen*, Artemis, IX, 543.

[11] Goethe, *Gespräche*, Artemis, XXII, 672–673. See also Goethe, *Gespräche mit Eckermann*, Artemis, XXIV, 399.

mechanical explanations of specific phenomena according to Democ-
ritus and the moderns—all of these elements you find united here in
one center of perspective.[12]

This is an impressive, indeed a proud, self-analysis of a
thinker who seems to have read "everything" and for that reason
commands a view of the "whole"—until the unexpected or un-
foreseen enters his vision. It befits the thinker who conceived the
formulation of a "characteristica universalis," a mechanical
model capable of projecting the probable course of a process,
including the possibility of deviation. Translated into the poetic
language of *Faust*, this is reflected in the universality of "striving," which carries with it the possibility of error.

In the subtle and scrupulous account of his own intellectual development Goethe remains surprisingly silent about Leibniz. Perhaps for reasons connected with his first exposure to
"Leibnizianism" at the University of Leipzig. Generally, we do
not associate Leibniz with a university. But his writings fell into
the hands of university teachers who made a method out of his
beliefs—the "enlightenment." As an intellectual system, rational-

---

[12] "Die Erwägung dieses Systems zeigt auch, daß man, wenn man den
Dingen auf den Grund geht, in den meisten philosophischen Sekten mehr
Vernunft entdeckt als man zuvor geglaubt hat. Die geringe substanzielle
Realität der Sinnendinge, die die Skeptiker, die Zurückführung aller
Dinge auf Harmonien oder Zahlen, auf Ideen und Perzeptionen, die die
Platoniker gelehrt haben; das identische allumfassende Eine des Parmenides und Plotin, das dennoch allem Spinozismus fernbleibt, die
stoische Notwendigkeit, die dennoch mit der Selbsttätigkeit verträglich
ist, die Lebensphilosophie der Kabbalisten und Hermetiker, nach denen
es überall Empfindung gibt, die Formen und Entelechien des Aristoteles
und der Scholastiker, die trotzdem die mechanische Erklärungsart aller
besonderen Phänomene gemäß Demokrit und den Modernen nicht aus-
schließen: dies alles findet sich hier wie in einem perspektivischen
Zentrum vereinigt . . ." See full quotation in Josef König, "Das System
von Leibniz," *Gottfried Wilhelm Leibniz: Vorträge der aus Anlaß seines
300. Geburtstages in Hamburg abgehaltenen wissenschaftlichen Tagung*,
ed. Hamburger Akademische Rundschau (Hamburg: Hansischer Gilden-
verlag, 1946), pp. 17–18.

ism was an educational theory or a program rather than a philosophy. It was concerned with the administration and management of the human mind. In such an atmosphere it was unlikely that Goethe would read Leibniz with any profit. What he did hear about him was repeatable *ad nauseam* and sufficient to kill any possible inquiry into the authentic origins of Leibniz's reasoning. Indeed the incipient image of Faust began to develop in his mind in strongest protest against "Leibnizian" rationalism.

Now, if the opening scene, reflecting Goethe's renewed effort toward the completion of *Faust*, the "Prologue in Heaven," contains distinct echoes of Leibnizian thought, namely, the culmination of the hierarchy of monads in the realm of Grace—how can such a reversal be made palpable? Scarcely by Goethe's renewed reading of Leibniz. Perhaps by the very subject and nature of his morphological studies which led Goethe into the proximity of the problem that had occupied Leibniz—the problem of movement, of growth and metamorphosis? Even this is uncertain. There is one theme, however tenuous, which brings the two thinkers together, and this theme is the justification of existence, the justification of its forms and un-forms, indeed the justification of "evil" and potential chaos in a system which is so obviously characterized by its orientation toward the "good" and toward harmony. In other words, it is the poetic symbolism of Mephistopheles.

With all its roots in the deepest and oldest layers of the human "soul," the figure of Mephistopheles injects the element of myth into the very midst of rationalism. Any visualization of Mephistopheles is beset by the risk of viewing him in *human* dimensions while, as a demonic principle, he is said to be "part of that force which, scheming Evil, accomplishes the Good." His configuration requires an infinite multitude of disguises; all of them point to the same principle: as the opposite of existence, he aims at the possibility of nonexistence. Happy were the times when a Dürer could picture a stalwart knight, riding on, unperturbed, even though he is stalked by the shades of a dreary Death and an ugly Devil. Faust's Devil demands more horrifying proportions: he demands the potentiality of disaster and the conceivability of negation. He has transcended the field of morality, as the tempter of persons, and has assumed more universal dimensions in that he foreshadows the void in uncanny transparency.

Human ambition reaches toward completion and synthesis. But completion and synthesis cannot be achieved without the consideration of contrast, opposition, negation. Any definition of one thing or state means the exclusion of others. A single, unique phenomenon—or monad—possesses its truth only insofar as it negates, or is itself limited by, the others and the whole. Negativity is the gap and the tension between the subject and the object, the vacuum that elicits motion; it is the difference between the individual and the general, and the reason for their relation and reconciliation. Negativity is the motivating force of differentiation and integration, the one function which discursive and symbolic thinking have in common.

But Goethe's *Faust* is no lesson in applied philosophy, and it would be inappropriate and unfair to assign to this piece of gorgeous poetry a primarily philosophical purpose. But when a considerable section of the play, in fact, one-eighth of the entire work, the tableaulike series of scenes known as the Classical Walpurgis Night, becomes transparent in a dialectical display of polarity, of antithesis and synthesis, then the analogy to philosophical thinking cannot be ignored, even if it is meant ironically. For these scenes demand of the reader "die Anstrengung des Begriffs" [the effort of conceptual reasoning]. This end becomes particularly evident when these scenes from which the poetic reincarnation of Helena—perhaps an aboriginal fertility figure—is supposed to result, turn out to be a symbolization of the *genesis of life* in which Mephisto plays the role of negativity. All along he has been playing that role. In the northern Walpurgis Night he turned up as the symbol of the destructive aspect of sexuality. It is he who knows the nature and the abode of the Mothers. He is the inventor of inflation. He has a share in the synthetic production of Homunculus. He has a share in the phantasmagoria which results in the second coming of Helena. Had Goethe lived in our day, Mephisto might have had a share in the making of the bomb and the pill. As a symbol of the reversibility of processes, Mephisto is the adversary *and* the implementer of *Steigerung*, the fundamental tenet of Goethe's philosophy. Even before Mephistopheles entered Goethe's poetic imagination, he aroused his fascination in the mythical image of Prometheus, the fire-demon; but it was an image in which the element of negativity and protest had been converted into an object of compassion.

With others of his time, then, Goethe shared the all-pervasive faith in progress. But this was more than the bland optimism which the educationist Enlightenment had made it appear. The very notion of *Steigerung* includes the absorption of potential discord. If by the time he planned the completion of *Faust* Goethe had come to a deeper understanding of Leibniz, he may have approached him through the medium of Spinoza, whom he knew well: he had learned to appreciate the peaceful atmosphere, the *Friedensluft*, which surrounded Spinoza's rationalist construct of *Deus sive Natura*, the reconciliation of opposites. This atmosphere is particularly noticeable in those portions of the text in which Goethe sought to integrate the *Faust* Fragment into the completed First Part; but these portions also abound with the elements of myth. And myth is the image of chaos at the beginning and at the end of time.

It seems significant that the structure of myth—if in this case we can speak about structure—points at chaos, disorder, and lack of orientation in two directions. The myth of chaos, as it was associated with the *Faust* legend through the hermetic tradition, possesses both past and future dimensions. It is based on the possibility of reversal: the myth lingering on at the horizon of the past still looms at the horizon of the future. Leibniz excluded any such concept of chaos, and so does Goethe, in the concluding scene of his play. Their vision of development is unequivocally forward—upward and on. And yet there is one token of doubt.

Goethe's sketchy plan of 1797, surprisingly, makes no allusion to the role of Mephistopheles. The terms "Lebens Genuß," "Thaten Genuß," "Schöpfungs Genuß" do not yield a hint as to what his function might be—except for the conclusion of the *Schema* which adds the enigmatic note: "Epilog im Chaos auf dem Weg zur Hölle" [Epilogue in chaos on the way toward Hell]. This note allows no possible reference to the completed text. It might become a starting point for another laborious inquiry into the relation between reason and myth. Is there the possibility of a reversal? the glint of a prospect or fear that the system of order that seems to underlie the universe might be running down? Or is there the possibility that at the limits of cognition reason has borrowed some aspects of myth—the view from within, the notions of totality and of cyclical recurrence —in order to conceal its own inadequacy? A comparison of Leibniz and Goethe, each in his own way symptomatic of the beginning and the end of the Age of Enlightenment, may reveal specific affinities, and doubtless many dissimilarities. Across their century they are united by the insight that no single concept, whether it be organism, symbol, structure, or form, can yield more than temporary knowledge unless it is projected into the perspective of a "dynamic" totality.

Romantic Neomythology

BY A. LESLIE WILLSON

The University of Texas at Austin

In the occasional jottings written down by Friedrich Schlegel while he served what he called his "philosophical apprenticeship," he notes in Jena in 1799: "Not only poetry but mythology is the approach to the sun."[1] It should not be surprising that a theoretician of literary aesthetics schooled in classical studies should so readily make an allusion to a familiar myth of Greece. Schlegel himself resembled a composite of Daedalus and Icarus, one the architect of the great labyrinth of Crete and the other the son who misused the wings his father built to escape the island. Schlegel's aphorisms thread

---

[1] Friedrich Schlegel, *Kritische Friedrich-Schlegel-Ausgabe*, vol. XVIII, *Die philosophischen Lehrjahre, erster Teil*, ed. Ernst Behler (Schöningh: Paderborn, 1963), p. 346. Further references to this edition are listed parenthetically as KFSA, with volume and page no. All are in my translation.

a labyrinthine way through the most varied realms of human thought, and at times his brilliant originality and prophetic perception lend him wings to escape the labyrinth. Often enough he lands safely from such flights, but then the Icarian side of his personality leads him, too, to venture recklessly close to impenetrable cores whose fierce heat brings him crashing down. *Lucinde*, Schlegel's multi-genred non-novel, had the fate of Icarus: a memorable flight, a tour de force, which ended in disaster; the novel pursued him ever after like the Furies. But Schlegel's "Gespräch über die Poesie" [Dialogue on Poetry], published in 1800 in the third volume of the Romantic journal, the *Athenaeum*, was a product of Daedalian genius, a daring and innovative demonstration, technically brilliant, flawlessly executed, and decisively significant in heralding the escape of Western literature from an impasse.

In the same jottings of 1799 Schlegel wrote: "Every age which *is* an age has its *own mythology*.—The goal of all art is to delineate it."[2] Convinced as he was that his own epoch was a significant time in the development of literature and art and philosophy and science, Schlegel was aghast that his epoch had no proper mythology. He realized that the lack of a viable, immediate mythology was symptomatic of a larger malaise which gripped the whole age. And he believed that the development of a new mythology would remove the symptom and help in the cure of the problematical malaise.

The problem which afflicted the age and which elicited Friedrich Schlegel's call for a new mythology is discussed briefly by Ernst Behler and Roman Struc in their introduction to an English translation of the *Dialogue on Poetry*, published in 1968. They allude to the pronouncements of that philosopher of history, Hegel, who, eight years after the first publication of the

---

[2] "Wie jeder höhere Mensch eine eigenthümliche Religion, so hat jedes Zeitalter, das ein Zeitalter ist, eine *eigne Mythologie*.—Diese darzustellen, ist das Ziel aller Kunst" (KFSA, XVIII, 344).

Dialogue, analyzed the history of European thought in a section of *The Phenomenology of Mind* entitled "Spirit." There Hegel traces the development of an awareness of Self which had come more and more to the fore in the ongoing process of human thought since ancient times: "From the objective and symbolical world of the Greeks, the Odyssey of the European spirit passed through the worlds of the Romans, of medieval Christianity, and rationalistic Enlightenment, until it came to a point where consciousness turned away from the objectivity of the outer world and plunged more and more into itself."[3] Hegel finds the beginnings of this inwardness in Kant's "recognition of the subjective foundation of human experience" (*Dialogue* [Introduction], p. 25) and he follows its development in Fichte's subjectivism. But the climax for Hegel is in literature and not in philosophy, in "the attitude of the Romantic artist who has transcended the objective boundaries of reality and consequently presents 'arbitrary subjectivity' in its purest form" (*Dialogue* [Introduction], p. 26), an attitude which Hegel frowningly calls the "declared evil." But Hegel's disapproval of the trend in no way enervated it, and he failed to recognize the new categories of reality which it produced.

Schlegel had perceived the plight of the artist in his own age. In essence, subjectivity had brought about the artist's "disrupted relationship to reality" (*Dialogue* [Introduction], p. 26). The great literary historian and critic Oskar Walzel stated the problem in his book *Poetry and Non-Poetry* in 1937 and is quoted as follows in Behler and Struc's Introduction to the *Dialogue*: "During the eighteenth century every firm and consistent world-view had been shaken too deeply to have left the indi-

---

[3] Ernst Behler, "Introduction" to Friedrich Schlegel's *Dialogue on Poetry*, trans. Roman Struc, with an Introduction by Ernst Behler (University Park: Pennsylvania State University Press, 1968), p. 25. Further references to this volume are listed parenthetically as *Dialogue*, with page no.

vidual poet a stable ideological foundation upon which to erect his literary work. His only recourse was to create for himself, by his own strength, a substitute for the stable world-view which formerly, and not only in antiquity, had been the un-questioned possession of the poet" (*Dialogue* [Introduction], p. 29). Schlegel's call for a new mythology in the central "Rede über die Mythologie" [Lecture on Mythology] from his *Dialogue on Poetry* was a bold challenge to his contemporaries, voiced strongly and with incontrovertible clarity, after fainter pleas by the "Magus of the North," Hamann, and then by Herder. Schlegel knew that the problem was not only an artistic one, but a philosophical, perhaps even basically a religious, one. The literary artist had effectively lost contact in a vital way with the world around him, and in his wake a large readership was foundering in a kind of literary limbo. A new mythology was necessary to transform, transfigure, and illuminate the dark and confused whorl of the objective world. Schlegel's aim was to reestablish contact with the objective world by urging the literary artist to create a new mythology which would combine the "*chaos* (of the outer world) with the *center* (of his inner being)" (*Dialogue* [Introduction], p. 28); which would, in other words, endow the objective world with form capable of being perceived in a higher and more expansive and compre-hensible way by man. This was the task which the new myth-ology had to perform.

It was a herculean task which Schlegel posed for all poets who came after him, and most immediately to those in the Jena circle—to Tieck and Novalis, above all. Every writer of stature had to become an Orpheus and quicken the objective world about him through the power of his own subjective creativity, while running the risk of the fate of Pygmalion—or of Orpheus himself. The new mythology become reality was not to be a panacea for the ills of all eras. Man's infirmities are everlasting, but the new mythology was to help him on his way, to sustain him in his unceasing effort to comprehend the world of nature and the community of men. Schlegel stated that "mythology is to be constituted through action."[4] The call to action in his "Lecture on Mythology" presents the categories and criteria for the creation of the needed new mythology.

Ludovico, the spokesman for Schlegel in the "Lecture," springs undaunted into immediate action, saying:

I will go right to the point. Our poetry, I maintain, lacks a focal point, such as mythology was for the ancients; and one could summarize all the essentials in which modern poetry is inferior to the ancient in these words: We have no mythology. But, I add, we are close to obtaining one or, rather, it is time that we earnestly work together to create one. . . . The new mythology . . . must be forged from the deepest depths of the spirit; it must be the most artful of all works of art, for it must encompass all the others; a new bed and vessel for the ancient, eternal fountainhead of poetry, and even the infinite poem concealing the seeds of all other poems.

You may well smile at this mystical poem and the disorder that might originate from the abundance of poetic creations. But the highest beauty, indeed the highest order is yet only that of chaos, namely of such a one that waits only for the touch of love to unfold as a harmonious world, of such a chaos as the ancient mythology and poetry were. For mythology and poetry are one and inseparable. . . . Everything interpenetrates everything else, and everywhere there is one and the same spirit, only expressed differently. (*Dialogue*, pp. 81–82)[5]

---

[4] "Mythologie *durch die That* zu constituiren" (KFSA, XVIII, 376).

[5] "Ich gehe gleich zum Ziel. Es fehlt, behaupte ich, unsrer Poesie an einem Mittelpunkt, wie es die Mythologie für die der Alten war, und alles Wesentliche, worin die moderne Dichtkunst der antiken nachsteht, läßt sich in die Worte zusammenfassen: Wir haben keine Mythologie. Aber setze ich hinzu, wir sind nahe daran eine zu erhalten, oder vielmehr es wird Zeit, daß wir ernsthaft dazu mitwirken sollen, eine hervorzubringen. . . . Die neue Mythologie muß . . . aus der tiefsten Tiefe des Geistes herausgebildet werden; es muß das künstlichste aller Kunstwerke sein, denn es soll alle andern umfassen, ein neues Bette und Gefäß für den alten ewigen Urquell der Poesie und selbst das unendliche Gedicht, welches die Keime aller andern Gedichte verhüllt.

Ihr mögt wohl lächeln über dieses mystische Gedicht und über die

Contained in these opening words are two essential qualities of
the new mythology: its origin in chaos and its undeniable unity
with poetry. That chaos is the beginning of being is a paradox
as ancient as the universe: The foundation of all order is disorder. It must be emphasized that chaos as Schlegel construes
it is not something negative, it is rather the source of all form
and substance, containing all things, as the Greeks understood
it (see *Dialogue* [Introduction], p. 11). Chaos has a symmetry
of its own, perceptible to those who ponder it creatively. In his
aphorisms and notes Schlegel links chaos and mythology. He
writes that "ancient mythology is obviously nothing but a
highly formed chaos.—The apotheosis of chaos."[6] His thesis
that chaos was a mythological concept (KFSA, XVIII, 352)
leads him to the insight that "Romantic poetry is related generally to chaos and mythology."[7] Ludovico is very specific:
"Romantic poetry . . . does not manifest itself in individual
conceptions but in the structure of the whole. . . . Indeed, this
artfully ordered confusion, this charming symmetry of contradictions, this wonderfully perennial alternation of enthusiasm
and irony which lives even in the smallest parts of the whole,
seem to me to be an indirect mythology themselves" (*Dialogue*,

---

Unordnung, die etwa aus dem Gedränge und der Fülle von Dichtungen
entstehn dürfte. Aber die höchste Schönheit, ja die höchste Ordnung ist
denn doch nur die des Chaos, nämlich eines solchen, welches nur auf die
Berührung der Liebe wartet, um sich zu einer harmonischen Welt zu
entfalten, eines solchen wie es auch die alte Mythologie und Poesie war.
Denn Mythologie und Poesie, beide sind eins und unzertrennlich. . . .
alles greift in einander, und überall ist ein und derselbe Geist nur anders
ausgedrückt." In Friedrich Schlegel, *Kritische Friedrich-Schlegel-
Ausgabe*, vol. II, *Charakteristiken und Kritiken I (1796–1801)*, ed. Hans
Eichner (Schöningh: Paderborn, 1967), pp. 312–313.

[6] "Die alte Mythologie ist offenbar nichts als ein höchst gebildetes
Chaos.—'Apotheose des Chaos' " (KFSA, XVIII, 326).

[7] "Die romantische [Poesie] bezieht sich durchgängig auf Chaos und
Mythologie" (KFSA, XVIII, 337).

p. 86).[8] There follows then a negative reference to "rationally
thinking reason" which might seem cause to hesitate: "This is
the beginning of all poetry, to cancel the progression and laws
of rationally thinking reason, and to transplant us once again
into the beautiful confusion of imagination, into the original
chaos of human nature" (*Dialogue*, p. 86).[9] It must be con-
fessed that the "Lecture" itself contains contradictions—but
contradictions and paradoxes are often useful for the understanding of higher truths. Ludovico's qualification of the word
reason with the reference to rational thought rescues it for the
poet. Later in the "Lecture," and elsewhere in his writings,
Schlegel emphasizes the role of reason in artistic creativity. In
the "Lecture" Ludovico also says: "Every hypothesis, even the
most limited, if systematically thought through, leads to hypotheses of the whole, and depends on such hypotheses even if without the conscious knowledge of the person who uses them"
(*Dialogue*, p. 90).[10] Chaos is a necessary ingredient in the creation of a new mythology. But there must be a unifying influence on chaos, the influence of the imposition of form on the
chaotic core of being, and such imposition of form makes use of

[8] "Da finde ich nun eine große Ähnlichkeit mit jenem großen Witz
der romantischen Poesie, der nicht in einzelnen Einfällen, sondern in der
Konstruktion des Ganzen sich zeigt, . . . Ja diese künstlich geordnete
Verwirrung, diese reizende Symmetrie von Widersprüchen, dieser wun-
derbare ewige Wechsel von Enthusiasmus und Ironie, der selbst in den
kleinsten Gliedern des Ganzen lebt, scheinen mir schon selbst eine indirekte Mythologie zu sein" (KFSA, II, 318–319).
[9] "Denn das ist der Anfang aller Poesie, den Gang und die Gesetze der
vernünftig denkenden Vernunft aufzuheben und uns wieder in die schöne
Verwirrung der Fantasie, in das ursprüngliche Chaos der menschlichen
Natur zu versetzen" (KFSA, II, 319).
[10] "Jede Hypothese auch die beschränkteste, wenn sie mit Konsequenz
gedacht wird, führt zu Hypothesen über das Ganze, ruht eigentlich auf
solchen, wenngleich ohne Bewußtsein dessen der sie gebraucht" (KFSA,
II, 324).

the reasoning power of the mind of the poet to create the unity
of poetry and mythology.

Schlegel seizes the opportunity in the "Lecture" to emphasize
the importance of the reestablishment of a unity in the most disparate areas of human intellectual activity and experience. A bi-
furcation had taken place in man's relationship to the world
about him. The split had been acknowledged by Schlegel, who,
in his development of Romantic irony, had sought intuitively to
imbue it with positive, transcendental qualities. But now Schlegel urges unity and coherence. Ludovico says, "In general, one
must be able to press toward the goal by more than one way.
Let each pursue his own . . . in the most individual manner; for
nowhere has the right of individuality more validity—provided
individuality is . . . indivisible unity and an inner and vital coherence—than here where the sublime is at issue" (*Dialogue*,
p. 87).[11] One goal of the new mythology was to give utterance
to the sublime—a goal which had not been achieved by philosophy or by poetry alone, but which now seemed capable of
attainment through creative, imaginative unity and coherence.

A synthesis productive of a new and illuminating objectivity
had to take place, and the new mythology was to be the catalyst
to effect such a synthesis. In effect, the search was for a new
kind of reality through literature. The contemporary philosophy
of idealism had served only to isolate man even more from his
surroundings. But the important part played by idealism in the
development of the new mythology was acknowledged by
Schlegel, and his Ludovico says:

If a new mythology can emerge only from the innermost depths of
the spirit and develop only from itself, then we find a very signifi-

---

[11] "Überhaupt muß man auf mehr als einem Wege zum Ziel dringen
können. Jeder gehe ganz den seinigen, . . . auf die individuellste Weise,
denn nirgends gelten die Rechte der Individualität—wenn sie nur das ist,
. . . unteilbare Einheit, innrer lebendiger Zusammenhang—mehr als hier,
wo vom Höchsten die Rede ist" (KFSA, II, 320).

cant hint and a noteworthy confirmation of what we are searching for in that great phenomenon of our age, in idealism. . . . Mankind struggles with all its power to find its own center. . . . Idealism in any form must transcend itself in one way or another, in order to be able to return to itself and remain what it is. Therefore, there must and will arise from the matrix of idealism a new and equally infinite realism, and idealism will not only by analogy of its genesis be an example of the new mythology, but it will indirectly become its very source. Traces of a similar tendency you can now observe almost everywhere, especially in physics where nothing is more needed than a mythological view of nature. (*Dialogue*, pp. 82–84) [12]

It might seem apparent that idealism was to turn in upon itself. But Schlegel did not believe in recurrence as a cyclical phenomenon, rather as a spiral. The same ground would not be trodden again. The line would rise in a progressive curve into new regions. Historical progress was a developing phenomenon, not simply reiterative echo. Subjectivism turned upon itself would not result in a more intense subjectivism but would enter new territories, would not compound itself but would explore other realms, would become objective in a miraculous way. Schlegel believed that the transition from subjectivism to the objectivism of a new mythology was inevitable in the course of history. Idealism, which was the culmination of the subjective spirit, formulated in Fichte's philosophy of the ego, was simply

[12] "Kann eine neue Mythologie sich nur aus der innersten Tiefe des Geistes wie durch sich selbst herausarbeiten, so finden wir einen sehr bedeutenden Wink und eine merkwürdige Bestätigung für das was wir suchen in dem großen Phänomen des Zeitalters, im Idealismus! . . . die Menschheit aus allen Kräften ringt, ihr Zentrum zu finden. . . . Der Idealismus in jeder Form muß auf ein oder die andre Art aus sich herausgehn, um in sich zurückkehren zu können, und zu bleiben was er ist. Deswegen muß und wird sich aus seinem Schoß ein neuer ebenso grenzenloser Realismus erheben; und der Idealismus also nicht bloß in seiner Entstehungsart ein Beispiel für die neue Mythologie, sondern selbst auf indirekte Art Quelle derselben werden. Die Spuren einer ähnlichen Tendenz könnt ihr schon jetzt fast überall wahrnehmen; besonders in der Physik, der es an nichts mehr zu fehlen scheint, als an einer mythologischen Ansicht der Natur" (KFSA, II, 313–315).

a stage in a dialectical transition to its contrary, a new objectivity, and, consequently, to a new view of the cosmos. Its immediate consequence was a new attitude toward nature, illustrated in the natural philosophy of Schelling (see *Dialogue* [Introduction], p. 27).

The relationship of idealism and mythology was not a notion conceived by Schlegel at the time of the "Lecture" in 1800. In his philosophical jottings four years previously he had written that mythology was the most absolute idealism (KFSA, XVIII, 90), and that all transcendental philosophy was mythology (KFSA, XVIII, 91). In the summation of the "Lecture," prepared for its republication in his collected works twenty years later, he reemphasizes the function of idealism in the creation of a new mythology, which would provide the ground for sublime realism and the unity of consciousness necessary for the creative, poetic imagination. "The beginning and the first impulse of the intellectual movement is contained in and furnished us by idealism, which in its own one-sidedness calls forth its opposite and leads again to that ancient system of unity which forms the true basis and the natural element of the productive power of the imagination, the source and matrix of all symbolic literature."[13]

Man's apprehension and comprehension of nature is essential for the new mythology. Ludovico links mythology and nature: "What else is any wonderful mythology but hieroglyphic expression of surrounding nature in this transfigured form of imagination and love?" (*Dialogue*, p. 85).[14] The most direct

[13] "Den Anfang und ersten Anstoß der intellektuellen Bewegung enthält und gewährt uns der Idealismus, der in seiner Einseitigkeit selbst den eignen Gegensatz hervorruft, und wieder zu jenem alten Systeme der Einheit führt, welches die eigentliche Grundlage und das natürliche Element der produktiven Einbildungskraft, der Quelle und Mutter aller symbolischen Dichtungen, bildet" (KFSA, II, 321). My translation.

[14] "Und was ist jede schöne Mythologie anders als ein hieroglyphischer Ausdruck der umgebenden Natur in dieser Verklärung von Fantasie und Liebe?" (KFSA, II, 318).

and miraculous revelations of nature came to the Romanticist in the scientifically all-embracing concept of physics. Ludovico continues:

I cannot conclude without urging once more the study of physics, from whose dynamic paradoxes the most sacred revelations of nature are now bursting forth in all directions. (*Dialogue*, p. 88)[15] . . . The energy of all the arts and knowledge meets at one central point, and I hope by the gods to be able to obtain nourishment for your enthusiasm even from mathematics and to kindle your spirit by its wonders. I preferred physics also for the reason that the connection here is most visible. . . . It is in fact wonderful how physics—as soon as it is concerned not with technical purposes but with general results —without knowing it gets into cosmogony, astrology, theosophy, or whatever you wish to call it, in short, into a mystic discipline of the whole. (*Dialogue*, p. 90)[16]

Joined now to mathematics and to physics, that is, to natural phenomena in their abstract and their material manifestations, is the important aura of religion, previously alluded to in reference to the power of mythology to give utterance to the sublime.

Religion hovers about the unity of the whole in reference to mystic discipline. But though there is a religious referent in Schlegel's new mythology, enhanced in the revision of the "Lecture" to include revelation itself, the religious focus resembles

[15] "Ich kann nicht schließen, ohne noch einmal zum Studium der Physik aufzufodern, aus deren dynamischen Paradoxien jetzt die heiligsten Offenbarungen der Natur von allen Seiten ausbrechen" (KFSA, II, 321–322).

[16] "Die Kraft aller Künste und Wissenschaften [begegnet] sich in einem Zentral-punkt, und [ich] hoffe zu den Göttern, Euch sogar aus der Mathematik Nahrung für Euren Enthusiasmus zu schaffen, und Euren Geist durch ihre Wunder zu entflammen. Ich zog die Physik aber auch darum vor, weil hier die Berührung am sichtbarsten ist. . . . Es ist in der Tat wunderbar, wie die Physik, sobald es ihr nicht um technische Zwecke, sondern um allgemeine Resultate zu tun ist, ohne es zu wissen, in Kosmogonie gerät, in Astrologie, Theosophie oder wie Ihrs sonst nennen wollt, kurz in eine mystische Wissenschaft vom Ganzen" (KFSA, II, 324–325).

true religion only in its emphasis on unity (see *Dialogue* [Intro-duction], p. 27). Further, Ludovico makes a point in regard to the sublime, with its religious connotations, which relates the new mythology to sound reason: "This is the crucial point: that in regard to the sublime we do not entirely depend on our emotions" (*Dialogue*, p. 85).[17] In one of his *Lehrjahre* note-books Schlegel expresses thoughts which relate the idea of God with reason and with myth, and further with a concept which is at heart the most important in the "Lecture on Mythology," with symbol: "All that which is material and indi-vidual in our intuition derives from the spirit. Every contact with the objective world liberates and makes visible, as it were, another piece of the Godhead which is latent in the intuiting subject. Thus, all that we intuit, we intuit in God. Therefore, everything is only a symbol, and nothing the meaning of which we can grasp is illusion" (*Dialogue* [Introduction], p. 18).[18]

One must concede that human intuition is fragmentary, a characteristic that in poetic intuition produced Romantic irony, which mirrors the conflict between the ideal and the real, deriv-ing from the poet's awareness of the necessity but the frustrat-ing impossibility of complete communication. This paradox—having to communicate but being unable to do so completely—leads the poet to endow his poetry with symbolic meanings in order to extend the boundaries of communication to their ex-treme limits. Schlegel challenges the poet's manipulation of symbol in his call for a new mythology, though the "Lecture" itself, in the version printed in the *Athenaeum* in 1800, makes

[17] "Das ist der eigentliche Punkt, daß wir uns wegen des Höchsten nicht so ganz allein auf unser Gemüt verlassen" (KFSA, II, 318).
[18] "Alles Materielle und Individuelle in der *Anschauung* kommt aus dem Geiste. Es wird mit jeder neuen Berührung des Objektiven gleichsam ein neues Stück der im Subjekt gebundenen Gottheit frei und sichtbar. Also was wir schauen, schauen wir Gott; darum ist alles nur Zeichen, nichts dessen Bedeutung wir verstehn nur Täuschung" (KFSA, XVIII, 171).

only the most casual use of the word *symbol.* In the 1823 revision of the "Lecture" in the fifth volume of his collected works,
Schlegel admits what he had become aware of as fact and what
can easily be inferred from the original "Lecture." Added to the
word *mythology* are such emendations as *symbolic art, symbolic
legend, symbolic world of ideas, symbolic knowledge,* and *a
symbolic science of the whole universe.*[19] An example of the
interpenetrability of the words *mythology* and *symbol* can be
read even in the original essay: "Mythology has one great advantage. What usually escapes our consciousness can here be
perceived and held fast through the senses and spirit like the
soul in the body surrounding it, through which it shines into
our eye and speaks to our ear" (*Dialogue,* p. 85).[20] Obviously
here mythology is synonymous with symbol. The manifold character of symbol is alluded to further: "Mythology is . . . a work
of art created by nature. In its texture the sublime is really
formed; everything is relation and metamorphosis, conformed
and transformed, and this conformation and transformation is
its peculiar process, its inner life and method" (*Dialogue,* p.
86).[21] This is a clear definition of the function and character of
symbol.

The importance, the necessity, the ineluctable presence of
symbol in poetic literature—couched in the first version of the
"Lecture" in terms of a new mythology—is unavoidable in the
second, revised version, which was Schlegel's acknowledgment

[19] Liselotte Dieckmann, "Friedrich Schlegel and Romantic Concepts of
the Symbol," *Germanic Review* 34 (1959): 276.
[20] "Einen großen Vorzug hat die Mythologie. Was sonst das Bewußtsein ewig flieht, ist hier dennoch sinnlich geistig zu schauen, und festge-
halten, wie die Seele in dem umgebenden Leibe, durch den sie in unser
Auge schimmert, zu unserm Ohre spricht" (KFSA, II, 318).
[21] "Die Mythologie ist ein solches Kunstwerk der Natur. In ihrem
Gewebe ist das Höchste wirklich gebildet; alles ist Beziehung und Ver-
wandlung, angebildet und umgebildet, und dieses Anbilden und Um-
bilden eben ihr eigentümliches Verfahren, ihr innres Leben, ihre Methode,
wenn ich so sagen darf" (KFSA, II, 318).

of what remained unspoken in the *Athenaeum* except symbolically in the term *a new mythology*. In the revised "Lecture"
Ludovico says: "In the case of the true poet all metaphors and
similes have a deep significance, and it would no doubt be rewarding and instructive if a natural philosopher, enlightened
in mind, were to extract this symbolism which lies concealed in
the images of poetry and bring it to light in an orderly fashion
as one great whole; or on the other hand, if an enthusiastic poet
of nature, not only unconsciously and with fortuitous instinct
but with consciousness, were to express in poetry that figurative
raiment of spring which as a thinker and visionary he recognizes in nature."[22]

The contours of the new mythology, revealed in essence as a
new concept of symbolism, revitalized and addressed to the
revelation of a unified, comprehensive, and progressive objectivism, begin to take shape. Those contours involve religion
(inclusive of a modern form of mysticism), history, philosophy,
science, and nature. There is one more source, which Schlegel,
in the persona of Ludovico, does not ignore, and that is the
immense body of myth and folk literature itself. He urges the
consideration of the mythologies of antiquity, adding to the
familiar troves of Greece and Rome the still largely unknown
treasures of the Orient, particularly of India (*Dialogue*, p. 87).
In the revision he expands the source of mythology even more,
including the Norse sagas and the folk tales of Arabia as well
as those of the West (KFSA, II, 320).

---

[22] "Bei dem wahren Dichter aber haben alle diese Bilder und Gleich-
nisse eine tiefe Bedeutung, und wohl wäre es lohnend und belehrend,
wenn ein im Geist erhellter Naturphilosoph diese Symbolik, welche in
den Sinnbildern der Poesie verborgen liegt, hervorzöge und als ein großes
Ganzes ordnend ans Licht zusammenstellte; oder auch von der andern
Seite, wenn ein begeisterter Naturdichter, nicht bloß unbewußt und aus
glücklichem Instinkt, sondern mit Bewußtsein, was er als Denker und
Seher in der Natur erkannt, nun in Poesie in jenem bildlichen Frühlings-
gewande aussprechen wollte" (KFSA, II, 320).

The neomythological program of Friedrich Schlegel did not spring full-blown from his fertile reflections. Notes from his philosophical apprenticeship furnish adequate evidence of the thought he had given to the concept of a new mythology. The breadth of the concept and its adumbrations and characteristics are clearly visible. Random selections of his thoughts from his philosophical notebooks can illustrate the tightly woven relationship of myth, or symbol, and the ingredients of the new mythology. To begin with religion, he believes that a book is a grammatical and mythological system—thus a religious concept (KFSA, XVIII, 78). He remarks that mysticism is native not only to theology, and he wonders if it should perhaps not be modern mythology: "Or should intellect form modern mythology?"[23] He concludes that ancient mythology, even the most ancient, can be explained mystically, although its originators did not intend it so, emphasizing the innate ability of mythology to transcend itself (KFSA, XVIII, 124). He links grammar and mythology in the production of poetry, commenting that literature is the work of religion *and* poetry, and finding that everything that is to a high degree religious and original has its own mythology and its grammar (KFSA, XVIII, 227–228). He probes for the very core of religion, suggesting that all religion is a combination of mysticism and mythology (KFSA, XVIII, 258). He suggests that mythology is the poetic form of mysticism (KFSA, XVIII, 346), and that mysticism is an inner mythology (KFSA, XVIII, 206). He stipulates that the great task is to transform ancient mythology into religion and Christianity into mythology (KFSA, XVIII, 400), and that taken together both mythology and religion equal poetry, projecting the innermost mystery of every human being (KFSA, XVIII, 465). Conjuring up visions of Dionysus and Isis he says that the

[23] "Oder sollte der Witz die moderne Mythologie bilden?" (KFSA, XVIII, 123).

ancient mysteries must now be made into mythology (KFSA, XVIII, 359).

Schlegel also places religion and mythology in close proximity to history, continuing then with the relationship of mythology to history. He states that the purpose of all art is to make our outward life divine, and that a vital depiction of religion equals mythology—interlocking with history (KFSA, XVIII, 404). Mythology is only the mystical part of history, he says (KFSA, XVIII, 231), and history and mythology must become one (KFSA, XVIII, 336). He is of the opinion that true popular philosophy must learn most from philology. This, and Romantic mythology, that is, what he defines as ethical poetry, are the essence of history (KFSA, XVIII, 77). In his book *Die Arabeske*, Karl Konrad Polheim points out that Schlegel demonstrates how history and poetry when taken together lead back to mythology.[24] He quotes a portion of a lecture delivered by Schlegel in Cologne in 1807: "The history of all nations leads us to mythology as the fountainhead of the art of poetry which, even though it is not a philosophical, artfully constructed allegorical universe, still makes reference to it always."[25]

The importance of philosophy in the delineation of the new mythology, especially the importance of idealism in the formulation of the concept of an objective but transcendental symbolism, was felt strongly by Schlegel. Repeatedly he alludes to the coherence of philosophy and mythology in his notebooks. He recognizes that the problems of modern philosophy are the often metamorphosed myths of ancient poetry (KFSA, XVIII, 130). His own visionary and prophetic qualities are comple-

[24] K. K. Polheim, *Die Arabeske* (Munich, 1965), p. 93. Further references to this book, with quotations in my translation, are given parenthetically as Polheim, with page no.

[25] "Die Geschichte aller Nationen führt uns auf Mythologie als Quelle der Dichtkunst, welche, wenn sie auch nicht ein philosophisches, künstlich gebildetes allegoristisches Universum ist, doch sich immer darauf bezieht" (Polheim, p. 126).

mented in his observation that oracle is the stuff of philosophy in the form of mythology (KFSA, XVIII, 300). His persuasion that myth is basic as a repository of human experience finds clear expression in the idealized statement that ancient mythology is the most beautiful and most profound philosophy and poetry about mankind (KFSA, XVIII, 327). He says that mysticism must appear as poetry (which would stress its symbolic function) and that mythology must appear as philosophy (KFSA, XVIII, 356).

Schlegel's reflections about philosophy led him to consider science, summed up for him in the concept of physics. He believed that through mythology and the perusal of nature, art and science would become poetry and philosophy (KFSA, XVIII, 335). The role of reason is considered in his statement that every science, every abstract system has its mythology (KFSA, XVIII, 97). Even the scientist becomes a sort of creative poet in an aphorism which holds that the methodology of the physicist must be historical—his ultimate goal mythology (KFSA, XVIII, 155). And the ultimate outcome of human endeavor seems to be speculated upon in the presumption that science and the arts will probably not resolve in religion, rather in poetry and mythology (KFSA, XVIII, 380).

The transition from science to nature came easily to Schlegel. He wanted to end the really unnatural and reprehensible separation of poetry and science in the coalescence of a new mythology. The initial move in that direction is glimpsed in the new technical language of physics. In a notebook entry of 1799 he writes: "The highest depiction of physics will necessarily be a novel. *Ideas of Mythology*: the fragments of the history of nature. But that is already mythology."[26] But though natural history and mythology are in a sense synonymous, he feels that the

[26] "Die höchste Darstellung der Physik wird nothwendig ein Roman. *Ideen der Mythologie*: die Bruchstücke von der Geschichte der Natur. Das ist aber schon Mythologie" (KFSA, XVIII, 155).

history of nature will be left to the age of a new mythology. Mythology seems timeless, for it must proceed into infinity (KFSA, XVIII, 153). He writes that his ideas about nature are precisely mythology, for the power of nature is the object of mythology (KFSA, XVIII, 358). In the revised "Lecture" Schlegel insists that, in poetry, metaphors from the realm of nature must not only be decorative, but must be symbolic in character, and must contain the symbolic features of nature itself. Metaphors from nature must consciously be imbued with symbolism by the poet.[27]

Schlegel addressed the makers of literature in his "Lecture." It took no great effort to realize that poets and writers are myth-makers, creators of symbol. Thus he was not apt to ignore the contributions of poets of the past (he alludes particularly to Dante, Cervantes, and Shakespeare) or the traditional corpus of mythopoeic literature. He defines allegory as artistic, mystic, philosophical, progressive myth (KFSA, XVIII, 81). The higher theory of poetry is contained in mythology (KFSA, XVIII, 354). He singles out fairy tales as being arabesques, mythological religion (KFSA, XVIII, 358). In his Cologne lecture of 1807 he contends that the mingling of very heterogeneous parts and even of all mythologies is a necessary task of the novel (Polheim, p. 200). And in a manuscript written in 1812 while he was in Vienna, Schlegel notes: "Mythical poetry belongs really by rights to the novel. . . . Folk fairy tale, legend, and novel also conform to mythology."[28] And, further, he says that novel, epic, elegy are the elements for the structure of mythological poetry (Polheim, p. 207f.). Schlegel continues in a similar vein with reference to the fairy tale, the romance, the idyll, and even lyric poetry. Again and again he accentuates the importance of ele-

---

[27] See Dieckmann, "Friedrich Schlegel," p. 282.

[28] "Die mythische Poesie gehört recht eigentlich zum Roman . . . An die Mythologie schließt sich auch das Volksmärchen, die Legende und der Roman an" (Polheim, p. 207).

ments of mythology—now understood properly as symbol—in creative literature.

Ernst Behler elucidates on the distinction Schlegel makes between exoteric and esoteric poetry in the journal *Europa* in 1802: "Exoteric poetry is classic poetry, . . . poetry on a small scale, which imposes art upon the world and in its depiction of the beautiful conforms to the proportions of form to which the human eye is accustomed. Esoteric poetry goes beyond man and seeks to embrace nature, the world, and man anew and to synthesize them in a new myth."[29] The distinction between exoteric and esoteric poetry might be said to be that between mere metaphor, however excellent, and stunning symbol. Further, Schlegel defines the relationship of symbol, or myth, and philosophical perception quite explicitly when he asks: "Is not mythology the idealistic treatment of the real?"[30] But beyond the unique gift poets possess, the symbol-making process is a gift shared by all mankind. There are simply degrees involved in this ability. A *Lehrjahre* aphorism of 1798 states: "Genius is the proper faculty of man, just as Novalis correctly interprets idealistic philosophy; namely that sound reason, general understanding, is nothing but the product of unconscious genius reduced 'to its lowest power' " (*Dialogue* [Introduction], pp. 16–17).[31] The best term to label this faculty is "creative

[29] "Die *exoterische* Poesie ist die klassische, gewissermaßen die kleine Poesie, welche die Welt verkünstlicht und sich bei der Darstellung des Schönen an die Formproportionen hält, welche das menschliche Auge gewöhnt ist. Die *esoterische* Poesie geht über den Menschen hinaus und sucht Natur, Welt und Mensch im ganzen neu zu umfassen und in einem neuen Mythos zu synthetisieren," Ernst Behler, "Der Wendepunkt Friedrich Schlegels. Ein Bericht über unveröffentlichte Schriften Friedrich Schlegels in Köln und Trier," *Philosophisches Jahrbuch der Görres- Gesellschaft* 64 (1955–1956): 245–271, here p. 258.

[30] "Ist Mythologie nicht die idealistische Behandlung des Realen?" (Polheim, p. 107).

[31] "*Genie* ist die reelle Kraft des Menschen, wie *Novalis* den *Idealismus* richtig ansieht, daß der gesunde Verstand, das allgemeine Denken Pro-

imagination," a talent innate in every man and observable in every child. But creative imagination raised to its highest power is the prerogative of the poet and may be called poetic imagination, that power of the poet to intuit the emanations of the Godhead and to express them symbolically (see *Dialogue* [Introduction], p. 17).

Reason is no stepchild to this indefinable process, but plays an ineffable role. Schlegel's new mythology is not the product of spontaneity but of reflection (see *Dialogue* [Introduction], p. 27). Reason is operative in the creation of symbol. Schlegel himself wrote in an aphorism: "Sagacity seems to be related to criticism, as reflection is to mythology."[32] In another aphorism he relates mythology and reason even more closely, as an essential chain in a cognitive, emanative process: "Love is the spark of the Godhead through which the universe becomes nature; and through reason nature returns back to the Godhead. —Perhaps the light will also finally be recognized only with mythology."[33]

To conclude this examination of the component parts of what Schlegel called a new mythology, of what he later admitted was a vital process of creative, symbolic acuity, here is one last aphorism from the portion of the philosophical notebooks written in 1799: "Mythology (as the central constituent between poetry and philosophy) cannot be the property of poetry alone, since philosophy also has its own.—When poetry and philosophy are one, then mankind will be one person. Perhaps then language itself will become mythology. . . . Works will then

---

dukt eines unbewußten Genies der niedrigsten Potenz ist" (KFSA, XVIII, 159).

[32] "*Scharfsinn* scheint sich auf Kritik zu beziehn, wie *Tiefsinn* auf Mythologie" (KFSA, XVIII, 106).

[33] "Die Liebe ist der Funke der Gottheit durch den das Universum zur Natur wird; und durch Vernunft kehrt die Natur wieder in die Gottheit zurück.—Vielleicht wird das Licht auch erst zuletzt erkannt werden mit Mythologie" (KFSA, XVIII, 153).

become chorales, and there will again be dialogues and discourses and history. The center will be mythology; then artists and other men will no longer be separated. Then also even nature, the universe, and the Godhead will flow together in this world."[34]

But that is not the end. The elucidation of the new mythology, of what turns out to be a grandiose call for a new symbolism, is but a prelude, a preamble, the merest outline. The "Lecture on Mythology"—and "Symbolic Perusal of Nature," as Schlegel enlarged the title in the second version—was, in its original form, a living force and presence in the literature of the period and has been a source of almost incalculable influence on German and other Western literatures ever since. The phrase *a new mythology* is a familiar one, though perhaps fraught with some mystery, contradiction, and hieroglyphic fascination. The phenomenal response to the call of Schlegel has been taken for granted and not analyzed, nor even reflected upon. But it is obvious that the first to answer the call, even as it sought formulation, was Novalis.

Novalis was the poetic genius among the early Romanticists, close friend and kindred spirit of Friedrich Schlegel, with whom he played the intellectual game of symphilosophy, or group philosophy. Like Schlegel, Novalis had a huge appetite for knowledge. He personified the transitional Romantic age, being himself a combination of efficient and expert administrator of salt mines and visionary poet of the highest quality. Like Schlegel, Novalis jotted down random thoughts, pithy frag-

[34] "*Mythologie* (als das Mittlere von Poesie und Philosophie) kann der Poesie nicht allein eigen sein, da ja auch die Philosophie die ihre hat.— Ist Poesie und Philosophie Eins, dann wird die Menschheit Eine Person. Vielleicht würde dann die Sprache selbst auch Mythologie. . . . Die Werke werden alsdann sein—Gesänge—Gespräche auch Reden und Geschichte wird es wieder geben. Das Zentrum wird Mythologie sein; dann werden Künstler und Menschen nicht mehr getrennt sein. Dann wird auch in der Welt selbst Natur, Universum und Gottheit zerfließen" (KFSA, XVIII, 255).

ments which sprouted like seedlings in the fertile imaginations of literary theorists and poets. He understood Schlegel's concept of a new mythology completely, as some of his notes indicate, in their similarity to those of Schlegel. The same dialectical interconnection of the subjective and the objective is evident.

Novalis advocated the mixture of the world of nature and the world of spirit in new, original fairy tales. Like Schlegel he advocated the novel as the literary vehicle to accommodate the mythological or symbolic task. He called the novel sovereign history, the mythology of history, as it were.[35] He maintained that prehistoric ages contained the dispersed features of the historical epochs which followed. The world of the fairy tale, he wrote, reflects the antithetical world of reality, of historical truth—and is for that reason so similar, just as chaos resembles in a paradoxical way the perfection of creation. In the world of the future everything will be as it was in the world of the past—though entirely different. "The future world will be rational chaos—chaos which has permeated itself, contained in itself and outside of itself, chaos to the second power or to infinity."[36] In his novel *Heinrich von Ofterdingen* Novalis demonstrates in the fairy tales told by Klingsor just what he meant. A chaotic world is depicted, a world in upheaval, brought to perfection through a fantastic intermingling of poetry, allegory, love, assorted myths, meteorological and cosmological phenomena, and chemical processes in mythical guise. It is true that reason is the villain of the piece, but it is reason in a cantankerous and meddlesome mood, not the higher and positive power of reason which operates with truth and proper order and with

[35] Friedrich von Hardenberg (pseud., Novalis), *Schriften*, vol. III, *Das philosophische Werk II*, ed. Richard Samuel (Darmstadt, 1968), p. 668. Further references are in my translation and are listed parenthetically as Novalis, III, with page no.

[36] "Die *künftige* Welt ist das *Vernünftige* Chaos—das Chaos, das sich selbst durchdrang—in sich und außer sich ist—*Chaos²* oder ∞ (Novalis, III, 281).

the flash of creative imagination. The entire procedure is eluci-
dated by Novalis in an aphorism: "Poetry heals the wounds
made by reason. For it consists precisely of opposite components—of sublime truth and pleasant illusion."[37] Schlegel, in the
journal *Europa*, indicated in 1802 that he was cognizant of
Novalis's contribution to the invention of a new mythology in
the novel. Referring to the mythological—that is, symbolic—
mingling of science and poetry, he believes that its perfection
will eventually be a great mythical novel, not in the style of
Goethe's *Wilhelm Meister* but rather in the style of Novalis's
monolithic fragment (see note 29).

Novalis shared other Schlegelian thoughts and applied them
poetically in a manner Schlegel himself could not do. He spoke
in aphorisms about the transformation of Christianity into modern myth (Novalis, III, 666–667); the Madonna had for him become mythical, that is, susceptible of transfiguration as poetic
symbol.[38] His *Hymns to Night* present the most varied admix-
ture of natural history, social history, intimate experience,
Greek mythology, and Christian myth, ending with a paean to
Christ and Mary become one androgynous symbol of love and
wisdom.

Most striking is Novalis's confirmation of the symbolic quality of myth and his discernment of the vital function of symbol
in literature. Symbol is really a concept of great complexity and
infinite possibility. He comments that every symbol can be further symbolized by what it symbolizes, forming counter-sym-
bols. Today the phrase *a Faustian spirit* has clear symbolic connotations. Further, he says that there are also symbols of symbols, that is, subsymbols (Novalis, III, 397). Today's man in

[37] "Die Poësie heilt die Wunden, die der Verstand schlägt. Sie besteht
gerade aus entgegengesezten Bestandtheilen—aus erhebender Wahrheit
und angenehmer Täuschung" (Novalis, III, 653).

[38] Novalis, *Schriften*, vol. II, *Das philosophische Werk I*, ed. Richard
Samuel (Darmstadt, 1965), p. 439.

the street knows very well what an Uncle Tom is. Of course, in the blue flower Novalis created the supreme symbol of Romanticism out of a confluence of natural history, legend, and Indic myth.

Finally, Novalis conceived of mythology as being related and applied in an absolute way through poetic metaphor to reality. Mythology is free, poetic invention, he said, which symbolizes reality in the most manifold fashion. His own works are a manifestation of the symbolic function of myth, and his erudition permitted him to make allusions to Arion, Orpheus, Isis, Christ, and Didymus. He mythologized the assorted fields of the physical sciences, exotic nature, philosophy, mathematics, literature, religions, and history to achieve their impressive and memorable transfiguration into symbol. To the Romanticist the ideal world, the unattainable but longed-for utopia, was epitomized in the concept of the golden age. Novalis wrote: "The golden age will have come when all words—*figurative words*—myths—and all figures—figurative language—will have become hieroglyphs, when one speaks and writes in figures."[39]

And suddenly, as though by magic, the literature of the West was shot through with electric sparks, galvanic mystery, automatons, ghoulish golems, mandrake roots, and mythological personages from literature and history. In Germany E. T. A. Hoffmann combined the worlds of reality and fantasy in *The Golden Pot*, a symbolic vision of the development of the poet in a hostile world. Friedrich de la Motte Fouqué conjured up the world of natural spirits in *Undine*. Heinrich von Kleist, in *Amphitryon* and *Penthesilea*, handed the ancient gods and heroic figures of Greece a new lease on life which has been renewed perennially ever since. The list could be amplified with examples from the works of Goethe, Wagner, Nietzsche, Haupt-

[39] "Das wird die goldne Zeit seyn, wenn alle Worte—*Figurenworte*—Mythen—und alle Figuren—Sprachfiguren—Hieroglyfen seyn werden—wenn man Figuren sprechen und schreiben—" (Novalis, III, 123).

mann, Thomas Mann, Hesse, and on down to the very present
hour. Illustrations from other literatures of the West could be
amply supplied. The whole symbolist movement has its often
obscure beginnings in the resultant mythopoeic creativity.

It would not be valid to say, and it would be impossible to
prove, that in his vision of a new mythology Friedrich Schlegel
singlehandedly elicited the burst of symbolic literature which
contains the constituent parts of his concept. It is more honest
to insist that Schlegel had insight into the currents of his own
epoch, that he glimpsed and had the audacity to describe the
dawn of symbol. But a brief recitation of some symbolic figures
in the literature of the West since 1800, grouped according to
the components of the new mythology, leave no doubt as to the
teeming fecundity of the age of symbolism and of the power of
the symbol to transcend itself: From religion, the literary re-
surrection of Christ, Buddha, Zoroaster, Joan of Arc, Pope
Gregory, who assume symbolic function; from history, the literary accommodation in symbol of the figure of the totalitarian
despot from Caesar past Caligula through Napoleon to Hitler,
of Thomas à Becket, of Columbus, of Henry the Eighth, of the
Marquis de Sade, of the sinister and nameless Grand Inquisitor,
of the unfortunate waif Kaspar Hauser, of the stolid English
symbol of the nineteenth century: Victoria. The list could be
continued with historic events summed up in a word: Waterloo,
the Alamo, Flanders, Lidice, Hiroshima, all of which have become symbolic, playing the role of myth in modern guise. From
philosophy and science, the ideas of Leibniz, Kant, Hegel,
Schopenhauer, Nietzsche, Freud, Jung, and a host of others. The
figures of such scientists as Pasteur and Oppenheimer, as well
as of such a monumental spirit as Galileo. Mention must also be
made of the products of the industrial revolution, from the Iron
Horse to the Gemini program, not to ignore the computer-pro-
genitor of Giles Goat-Boy (the titular hero of the novel by John
Barth). From nature, the processes of chemistry and physics,

as well as natural and supernatural phenomena, including the ubiquitous elemental spirits, and more recently the double-helix, the Andromeda strain, and Aquarius. And from literature itself, as testimony that the poets and writers of all times have proven to be infinitely inventive and original, the creations of Shakespeare, Dickens, Hardy, Kafka, and such fictional characters as Robinson Crusoe, Frankenstein, Don Quixote, Faust, Don Juan, and the mythological figures of the Greeks and Hindus and Norsemen and Egyptians. Acknowledgment of the characters of folk fairy tales must be made, a recent example being Donald Barthelme's communal Snow White. The list could be continued interminably in every category, and an encyclopedia of symbol would result in a modern, a *new* mythology.

Friedrich Schlegel was not only the first to perceive the crisis in poetry in the late eighteenth century, he was also the first to anticipate and prophesy the solution to the quandary in which creative writers wallowed. Of course, it must be admitted that poets in ages before him had made memorable use of symbol in the creation of characters which transcended themselves, such as the knight of the woeful countenance and the melancholy Dane. It is true that in the original "Lecture," in 1800, Schlegel did not think consciously in terms of symbol, an omission which he corrected fully in the revised "Lecture" of 1823. But in his use of the phrase *a new mythology* he coined a symbolic referent himself. He knew myth. He had pondered myth. He was quite aware that the function of myth is to make it possible for man to relate to the world around him in a symbolic and revelatory way. And because of the hypersensitive awareness of Self induced by transcendental idealism, Schlegel knew also that the result of the function of myth, or symbol, would be the establishment of a new objectivism, a process which transcends and enhances the reality which is but imperfectly perceptible to man through his senses and ordering reason. With his new mythology Schlegel proposed a path to a metareality.

The goal of Friedrich Schlegel's quest for a new mythology was poetic in the largest sense, but beyond literature was the literary experience itself in the response of the reader. Through the symbolic event the mind of the reader expands to receive an awareness, a recognition of a transcendent reality, a metareality perceived through symbol. The process—and the new mythology—seems unending. But the voyage to the sun is long and hazardous. Perhaps we can be content for the nonce simply to escape the labyrinth.

Treasure and the Quest for the Self in Wagner, Grillparzer, and Hebbel

BY LEE B. JENNINGS

The University of Illinois at Chicago Circle

I shall proceed on certain basic assumptions: first, that myth is a system of archetypes denoting a process, with the potentiality of magically enhanced significance. Since most processes can be expressed in terms of growth, decline, and sudden transformation, the central myth is that of death and rebirth. Further, since C. G. Jung has been most successful in identifying and explaining the meaning of archetypes, his theories must be taken as a starting point in any work in this field. I assume further that Jung was correct in his belief that there is a parallel between individually conceived archetypes and those of the culture or the age, and that, as a result, visionary inventions of the individual artist may have a bearing on the problems of the day, and, conversely, collective and popular myths always have a significance in terms of individual psychic development. For the sake of simplicity, I shall refer to this phenomenon for our purposes as the "psychohistorical parallel."

Wagner's *Ring des Nibelungen* (1848–1874), Grillparzer's *Das goldene Vließ* (1818–1820), and Hebbel's *Nibelungen* (1855–1860) are all monumental attempts to adapt mythical material to nineteenth-century ends. All have at their core a basic myth: the winning of treasure from the clutches of a dragon or serpent by a hero, and, in addition, all portray the downfall or decline of the hero and the emergence of a powerful female figure.

Of the three treatments, Wagner's is obviously the most individualistic. Whatever one may think of his ponderous pathos and overwrought heroism, he is the most successful creator of a new mythology in his day. It should not surprise us, therefore, if archetypal patterns emerge in his *Ring* cycle, and, in fact, Donington has provided a detailed Jungian interpretation of them.[1] I shall therefore only briefly sum up Donington's findings in order to see whether they may be used as a paradigm in our approach to the other two works, which, though less original, nevertheless show surprising parallels in the use, or obtrusion, of visionary material.

According to Donington, the Nibelungen treasure has two levels of significance. Basically, it is libido, the life energy, which can be turned to external or internal purposes and in the latter case provides the means for psychic development. In a higher sense—especially in its ring form—it is the symbol of deep individual worth and thus tends to be equated with the self, the central orientation point of the psyche and at the same time its totality, the summation of conscious and unconscious components. The gold "has to do with that slow, life-long growth in a man's character by which he draws away from the collective unconscious of mother nature and acquires an increasing awareness of his own individuality in its deepest sense,

[1] Robert Donington, *Wagner's Ring and Its Symbols* (New York: St. Martin's Press, 1963).

so much deeper than his ego alone" (p. 54). The treasure is immersed in water and guarded by chthonic dwarfs or elves; that is, the potentiality for self-fulfillment lies in the bonds of the unconscious, the infantile mother-realm from which it is to be rescued. Alberich, Mime, and Hagen, who seek to lay claim to the ring at a lower stage of its progress, are representatives of the shadow archetype, basically a regressive figure, but one who, since he underlies the conscious ego as its inferior counterpart, must be confronted in the interests of greater awareness of the unconscious, if psychic integration is to be achieved. Feminine figures, on the other hand, are likely to assume attributes of the more profound anima archetype, the contrasexual substratum of the male ego and symbol of the soul. The anima may act as a spiritual guide in the integration process. At the lowest end of the developmental process the anima may merge with the grandiose and mythic Magna Mater, or Earth Mother, the source of individual consciousness (symbolized by the hero) and the power that seeks to reclaim it and halt its growth. Or, at the higher stages, the anima may acquire the status of a god-like self symbol, Sophia or the Mater Gloriosa. Erda, as anima mundi, seems to waver between these superhuman variants. The more common appearance of the anima, however, is that of the soul mate, who is at once bride, sister, alter ego, guide, and mother. Fricka fills this role for Wotan, Sieglinde for Siegmund, and Brünnhilde for both Siegfried and Wotan. Marriages, especially incestuous ones, are likely to symbolize the conjunctio oppositorum, the union of conscious and unconscious factors, and, like the various representations of rebirth, this points to the experience of transformation, the death of the ego and its identification with the higher, broader, or deeper ideal of the self, and its emergence as something closer to the self. Deaths, notably that of Siegfried, may likewise be symbolic of ego death, though this does not preclude a realistic acceptance of mortality and suffering.

Wotan is the central figure in the psychic drama. As a personage in his middle years, he has spent his life in the extraverted activity of building Valhalla. Though godlike figures usually symbolize the Self, he appears to stand for the ego. His egoistic one-sidedness causes him to exclude tenderness from his domain (Freya and her golden apples). He must now muster his strength in the form of the successive hero archetypes Siegmund and Siegfried in order to seize the sword of his destiny and to reclaim that gold which makes psychic transformation possible. The watery prepsychic world of innocence gives way to the water-and-cave world of elves, giants, and dragons, a more sinister realm because it is more eventful. The chicanery of Wotan and Loge (the trickster archetype, a variant of the shadow) is not to be taken too seriously in this mythical setting. Through the guidance of Fricka, Brünnhilde, and Erda (who, to be sure, give conflicting advice, as anima figures are likely to do), Wotan finally comes to the realization that he must acquiesce in his own destruction, bowing to his creation, Siegfried, thus willing his ego-death in order to emerge transformed as Siegfried. In forcing Brünnhilde into exile, Wotan forces his anima into the world of the shadow, the same fault Siegfried commits in his unknowing desertion of Brünnhilde for Gutrun. Siegfried, too, must throw his life away—as he symbolically does shortly before his murder—in a gesture of transformation. The ego, in its involvements with the feminine principle of its own unconscious, precipitates catastrophes, but these catastrophes further growth. The rising arm of the dead Siegfried assures the ascendancy of the spirit.

Finally, Brünnhilde's self-sacrifice, with its mystic union of fire and water and of herself with the departed Siegfried, is, according to Donington, yet another symbolic transformation designed to redeem the gods, that is, the psyche. This, Donington admits, is in contrast to Wagner's Schopenhauerian view that the sacrifice signifies freedom from rebirth, but he feels with some justification that the symbols tell their own story.

If the Jungian interpretation sometimes seems superfluous, it is because Wagner, in his instinctive grasp of archetypal patterns, elaborates the meanings so clearly himself—though, as Donington believes, his insights were of no great use toward his own mental well-being, art being achieved once more at the expense of life. Still, Jung's categorization of the phenomena provides us with a tool for approaching other visionary and mythical products.

There remains one point to be clarified, however. Wagner himself seems to supply broad hints, especially in Alberich's elaborate curse upon the ring and in Erda's final altercation with Wotan, that Wotan's striving is reprehensible, since it represents unscrupulous egoism and power-seeking, while the gold easily lends itself to an equally reprehensible materialistic greed. The discrepancy between this and the more favorable Jungian interpretation is not as great as it might seem, however. The liberation of libido from the infantile realm of mother-domination, symbolized by Wotan's destruction of the sacred ash and his fashioning of the spear-staff with inscribed contracts, will of necessity be impetuous and cruel, and the new-born ego will have to undertake successive reorienting transformations characterized more and more by self-abnegation and inward looking.

Then, too, Wagner, having an instinctive grasp of the archetypes but little overt understanding of them, may have felt the need to overlay his myth-play with a more conventional ethically oriented tragedy of hybris and nemesis. Further, we can note in all of our authors the prevailing pessimism with regard to human aspiration, the extreme deprecation of covetousness and egoism for which Schopenhauer is symptomatic. Ego was seen as a rigid and inexorable entity, and knowledge that it

might broaden itself in small stages by the assimilation of unconscious material lay in the future. The only remedy was
resignation, self-abnegation, or utter transfiguration. Thus, the
residual ominous quality inherent in mythical treasures—probably a symbolic warning against releasing the energies of the
unconscious to the service of an intransigent and static ego—
is seized upon and exaggerated in the post-Napoleonic era.
Perhaps the lesson learned from Napoleon was learned too well.

Grillparzer was aware of the grandiosity of the Jason-Medea
theme and had some misgivings about undertaking a treatment
of it. Later, he felt that in his trilogy he had indeed somewhat
overstepped the bounds of his special talents. The particular
attraction for him lay in the figure of Medea, with its attendant
problems of motivation, and in the motif of the Fleece itself,
which he regarded in retrospect as a kind of *Nibelungenhort*,
though at the time of writing that was not a prevalent concept.[2]
The Fleece is thus clearly intended to be a central, symbolic
motif, and we may well conjecture that a myth, vividly revived,
has once again acquired both personal and universal significance in a particular time and place. In an epilogue intended to
be recited after the first part of his trilogy, Grillparzer tells us,
in strangely obscure pronouncements, that the content of this
serious play is really man's origin and end, as well as the forces
concealed within his breast and the forces that conceal his
breast from him.[3] To be sure, Grillparzer also warned against

[2] See Grillparzer's "Selbstbiographie," in his *Sämtliche Werke*, ed. Peter
Frank and Karl Pörnbacher (Munich, 1965), IV, 87–88 and 113–114;
ibid., I, 1310–1311. This edition is hereafter abbreviated: *SW*. The wording is of interest: "Das goldene Vließ war mir als ein sinnliches Zeichen
des ungerechten Gutes, als eine Art Nibelungenhort, obgleich an einen
Nibelungenhort damals niemand dachte, höchst willkommen."
[3] "Von wo der Mensch beginnt, womit er endet,/ Und was für Mächte
in der Brust verbirgt,/ Und was für Mächte seine Brust ihm bergen,/ Das
ist der Inhalt unsers ernsten Spiels" (*SW*, I, 137–138). The additional

interpretations which would try to make of the Fleece something more mysterious than a concrete incorporation and emblem of the dictum that the evil deed must continually beget further evil.[4] Even the older critics, however, suspected that he was on the defensive against charges of fatalism made against him since his *Ahnfrau* [The Ancestress].[5] He seems to have been temporarily blinded to the fact that an air of fate need not merely further sensationalism and cheap theatrics, but that it may underline a profound and universal significance.

Grillparzer's later attitude of distaste toward his *Ahnfrau* may, in fact, not be irrelevant to our theme. It has been suggested that the ancestral ghost is in part a representation of the vicious archetypal mother who thus reclaims the weak and autobiographical hero Jaromir as her own.[6] If, in this play, Grillparzer investigated the anima in its wicked-mother phase, the later play *Der Traum ein Leben* [The Dream: a Life] can be considered his encounter with the shadow. In so far as the work is to be identified with Grillparzer's own fantasy product, we may conclude that he misapprehended the message being conveyed to him by his own organism. Instead of learning from the Mephistophelean Zanga that greater outward enterprise might be called for, even at the expense of strict ethics, he drew the opposite conclusion: that the *vita activa* is to be shunned (providing, of course, that Rustan's conclusions are to be regarded as Grillparzer's own).

Das goldene Vließ, then, can be considered one of a series of plays in which Grillparzer attempts half-unconsciously to come

---

connotation of *bergen* [protect for], alongside "conceal from," is equally compatible with the concept of repression.

[4] Reinhold Backmann, "Vom Werdegang des goldenen Vließes," in *Grillparzer-Studien*, ed. Oskar Katann (Vienna, 1924), p. 176.

[5] Backmann, *Studien*, pp. 175–176.

[6] Egbert Krispyn, "Grillparzer and His *Ahnfrau*," *Germanic Review* 38 (1963): 209–225.

to terms with archetypes of great personal meaning, and his
disclaimer of the Fleece's deeper significance need not be taken
at face value. This work, too, has its quite legitimate air of fate,
and we might indeed speculate whether this does not invariably signal the regressive victory of the Magna Mater.

Grillparzer says elsewhere that the Fleece is a concrete sign
of that which is desirable, ardently sought, and unjustly acquired; or rather, he says that he has attempted to make it this,
and that his drama will stand or fall with the degree of his success.[7] While it is true that mythical treasures always have something sinister about them, true, too, that in this case even the
ancient sources never really made it clear why the Fleece is
desired and what it is good for, we are still struck by Grillparzer's overriding stress on the negative side. No one, not even
Medea, seems to benefit much by its possession. Aietes realizes
in mid-grasp that it is a dubious acquisition; and the best justification Jason can bring forward for wanting it is that it is a
token of the Greeks' well-being and fortune. Ambiguity sur-
rounds it; no one seems to have an unencumbered claim upon
it, so that the idea of its being "ill-gotten" becomes virtually
meaningless. It is even in doubt that Phyrxus stole it from
Delphi; according to his story, the strange troglodytic god
Peronto bequeathed it to him in a dream. The repeated statement that it brings with it "victory and revenge" is likewise
ambiguous—victory for whom, and revenge upon whom for
what? An ironic meaning is suggested by the tendency of the
Fleece's owners to think that both victory and revenge will be
theirs, whereas the revenge is sometimes exacted upon them.
Since, in the natural course of events, all of them can be called
victorious in some undertaking, and since no one escapes some
kind of revenge, it is difficult to pinpoint the exact role of the

---

[7] "Ein sinnliches Zeichen des Wünschenswerten, des mit Begierde
Gesuchten, mit Unrecht Erworbenen . . ." (Diary entry of 1822, SW, IV,
380).

Fleece. The only concrete manifestation of its power seems to be its ability to call up the image of a murder victim in Kreon's case, but this is also questionable. Van Stockum has shrewdly and laconically summed up the symbolism of the Fleece in Grillparzer's treatment as a combination of nemesis and that force which Schopenhauer calls "will to live" and Nietzsche calls "will to power."[8] Most interpretations have merely re-named the aspects mentioned by Grillparzer himself, stressing now the demonic lure of the prize, now its apparently baneful effects (or its symbolization of such baneful qualities as power and greed).[9]

Donington's findings with regard to Wagner can be applied here. The Fleece, like all ardently coveted treasures of myth-ology, represents libido and aims at the concept of Self. In view of Grillparzer's highly inhibited personality, his inability or un-conscious unwillingness to win or accept the prizes of life, it is not surprising that he should stress the negative aspects of the treasure so strongly. For him, all gains are "ill-gotten," all goals elusive. His Fleece can be considered the ultimately satisfying goal of Schopenhauer's will—a spectral object, since this goal is actually nonexistent.

Thus, because of his prejudice against action and goal-seeking, Grillparzer again seems to miss what might be a profit-able message inherent in an archetypal motif: that life-energies, properly channeled, can overcome psychic stagnation and pro-mote development toward greater spirituality, rather than be-ing detrimental to it. The *vita activa* and the *vita contemplativa*

---

[8] Th. C. Van Stockum, "Grillparzers Medea-Trilogie 'Das goldene Vließ' (1818–1820) und ihre antiken Vorbilder," *Neophil.* 47 (1963): 120–125.

[9] See Herbert Seidler, " 'Das goldene Vließ': Forschungslage und In-terpretationsaufgaben," in *Grillparzer-Forum Forchtenstein*, 1966, pp. 64–77; and Rudolf Stiefel, *Grillparzers "Goldenes Vließ": ein dichterisches Bekenntnis* (Bern, 1959).

are best not regarded as irreconcilable opposites, but as Yang and Yin, complementary and mutually fruitful principles.

Perhaps wishing to avoid an excess of the fantastic, Grillparzer omits to mention the most common ancient account of the origin of the Fleece as the hide of a miraculous talking and flying ram, an unmistakable symbol of the male principle of *Geist*, or Logos.[10] The omission may have its reasons, since Grillparzer would be expected to overlook this upward-looking symbol of spiritual and intellectual growth and to stress instead chthonic mother imagery, and he does this to a remarkable degree in his vivid presentation of the labyrinthine serpent's cave of Colchis which is undoubtedly the true home of the Fleece. Colchis is also clearly the realm of the unconscious, where unfathomable forces are at work and where, as Jason never tires of repeating, all our usual standards and guidelines go awry. Greece, on the other hand, is the world of reason, intellect, and deliberate endeavor, in other words, the conscious ego. The work revolves about the conflict between the two. Grillparzer makes this clear when he makes this basic conflict the justification for his use of Romantic as well as classical style.[11]

In its thwarted masculine aspect, of course, the Fleece is a symbol of the Greeks' and Jason's power and prowess; and Jason's gradual decline in vigor and enterprise, his development of peevish and hypersensitive traits, stamp him as the archetypal hero whose quest has failed. His reclaiming by chthonic forces is accompanied therefore by an actual or symbolic castration. Grillparzer supplied the detail of Medea's returning the Fleece to Delphi as an afterthought, but one which seemed to add the finishing touch to his work.[12]

---

[10] The Fleece is specifically referred to in Grillparzer's drama as a ram's hide, however; and the head of the ram is clearly discernible in Grillparzer's own weirdly phallic pen sketch for the closing scene of *Die Argonauten* (see Backmann, *Studien*, opp. p. 164).

[11] "Selbstbiographie" (*SW*, IV, 89, 110–111).

[12] Backmann, *Studien*, p. 170.

In the rise to power of Medea we could scarcely ask for a clearer representation of the anima partly split off from its wicked-mother phase but reverting back to it. The overpowering of the hero by the chthonic forces is of course given in the sources and is hardly avoidable in the dramatic treatment. It is no accident, however, that Grillparzer was attracted to this theme at this time in his life.

Two events have long been recognized as being in some way related to the origin of the work: the suicide by hanging of Grillparzer's mother (strangely transmuted in his autobiographical sketch to a natural death—while standing up) and his romantic involvement with Charlotte von Paumgarten, the wife of his cousin, to whom the work was found to be dedicated, under the name of "Desdemona," in a posthumous document.[13] Either or both of these events, both perhaps tinged with incestuous guilt, contributed to a severe mental crisis and a lengthy interruption of the work.

On taking up the work again, Grillparzer tells us, he was able to recapture his creative lines of thought by a strange device. He had been accustomed to play four-handed piano arrangements of the classical symphonies with his mother while musing about his dramatic work. Now, after her death, the embryonic ideas began coming back to him only when he again played the same arrangements with a lady acquaintance.[14] This is a striking confirmation of the role of the anima as muse, functioning to release the libido and to bring about a streaming of inner energy.

As regards the adulterous involvement with Charlotte von Paumgarten, its importance is best summed up by a contemporary poem, "Der Bann" [The Spell], in which the poet sees himself doomed by his choice of art over life to a restless ex-

[13] SW, I, 971; IV, 90.
[14] "Selbstbiographie" (SW, IV, 106–107).

istence of shadow-chasing. Thus, Grillparzer takes refuge in the argument of temperament and vocation to explain why he has not sought and found life's treasures.[15] In a like vein, in his poem "Märchen," the poet-as-knight fails to gain the treasure, that is, beauty, from the guardian dragon and eventually gives up.

Grillparzer's work interruption first took the form of a creative block involving the early scene of awakening love between Jason and Medea. Try as he would, Grillparzer could not bring them together; Medea's betrayal of her father hung over her too heavily; the Amazon in her tended to predominate; and a paean to love by Jason (oddly, one built upon Plato's hypothesis of an original androgynous being) was manifestly out of character.[16]

Grillparzer, perhaps dimly aware of the significance for him of his mythical material, shied away again from its message: the profitable union of male and female principles, in which, at this juncture, an ascendancy of the masculine was called for. The principles remain separate, even in their nominal union. Medea continues to exude the miasma of Colchis. Jason, while decidedly masculine, is the prototype of the egoist, stagnating as the ego always stagnates when its union with the unconscious is only nominally consummated. Grillparzer, being only too cognizant of the pitfalls awaiting such a type as Jason, was sometimes unable to recognize the Jason within himself and to see that Jason's problem was also his, turned a different way.

This is not to say that the aesthetic success of the work hinges upon the successful resolution of a mental conflict either on the part of the author or openly or symbolically within the work. There is a place for the work lamenting failed integration. Yet, too great a psychic stagnation on the author's part may leave its mark on the work in the form of aridity and tedious lugubriousness. In view of Jung's psychohistorical parallel, it is interesting

15 SW, I, 1310, 109–111.
16 Backmann, Studien, pp. 146–157.

to speculate that the symbols of flawed development and stagnation in Grillparzer's drama may have had broader cultural
parallels. It has indeed been suggested recently that Grillparzer's Greece is equivalent to the Hapsburg empire whose
decline the poet clairvoyantly foresaw.[17]

Hebbel's similarly ambitious attempt to create a monumental
drama from a semimythical source comes some forty years later.
By that time, the *Nibelungenlied* had come to be regarded as
the national German epic, and Hebbel was no doubt motivated
by a sense of patriotic obligation as well as by the challenge
presented. What a boon it would be for the nation, he muses, if
the dramatic Nibelungen treasure were finally raised;[18] and
when he finally attempts the task himself he admits to modest
glimpses of the magical trophy.[19] His description of the medieval *Nibelungenlied* as a "deaf-and-dumb poem that speaks
only through signs"[20] suggests that he was attracted also to the
archetypal patterns in the work. Personal psychological involvement is also probable: in a letter elaborating upon the
point that all of his dramatic subject matters are happened on
by chance, he specifies a performance of Raupach's Nibelungen
play, in which his wife played Kriemhild, as the stimulus in this
case.[21] In his prologue to the cycle he tells how this experience
revived in his memory the figures of the *Nibelungenlied* which

[17] Piero Rismondo, "Das 'zweite Gesicht' in Grillparzers 'Das goldene
Vließ,'" in *Jahrbuch der Grillparzer-Gesellschaft* (Vienna, 1966), ser.
3, vol. 5, pp. 129–141.

[18] Friedrich Hebbel, *Sämtliche Werke*, ed. Richard Maria Werner (Berlin, 1904–1907), referred to hereafter by volume and page of each of its
independent subdivisions, *Werke, Tagebücher*, and *Briefe*: (*Werke*, XII,
21). References to some specific passages of *Die Nibelungen* are given
by line number.

[19] *Tagebücher* IV, 101, entry no. 5537.

[20] "Ein taubstummes Gedicht, . . . das nur durch Zeichen redet" (*Tagebücher* IV, 59, entry no. 5405).

[21] *Briefe* VII, 302–304.

had fascinated him when, as a child, he pored over the book and felt that he was listening at a magic fountain.[22] It is true that he sticks quite closely to the twelfth-century text, and it might be questioned whether his psychological involvement is, under the circumstances, demonstrable or significant. His creative birth pangs seem to have been no less intense than for any of his other works, however. He speaks of working with febrile fervor,[23] and his description of his procedure is indicative of anything but a dry intellectual approach; he can no more prepare for the creative task, he says, than one would prepare for a dream; rather, he sees figures in the twilight of his fantasy and seeks to capture them as a painter would. One figure after another emerges, and the rest present themselves when they are needed.[24]

Further, the changes Hebbel makes are not always occasioned by the demands of dramatic technique, as he would have us believe at other times. He is, quite naturally, at pains to create a sharply outlined continuum of realistic motivation in a twelfth-century setting, and it is clear that the magical elements have to be eliminated from this continuum as significant agents. In keeping with his usual procedure, he introduces conflicting older and newer ideologies within this continuum to give some historical perspective within the period.[25]

The mythical and magical elements are then reintroduced,

[22] *Werke* IV, 5–6.

[23] *Tagebücher* IV, 151, entry no. 5774.

[24] *Tagebücher* IV, 148, entry no. 5767. Mörike's reaction to Hebbel's drama, as Hebbel reports it: the feeling that a large block of stone had fallen through the roof (*Tagebücher* IV, 237–238, entry no. 6038) should make us wary of neglecting its primitive impact.

[25] See Helmut de Boor's Introduction and appendices to Hebbel's *Nibelungen* in Ullstein's "Dichtung und Wirklichkeit" series (Frankfurt am Main & Berlin, 1966), esp. pp. 19–37. See also Jost Hermand, "Hebbels 'Nibelungen'—Ein deutsches Trauerspiel," in *Hebbel in neuer Sicht*, ed. Helmut Kreuzer, 2d ed. (Stuttgart, Berlin, Cologne, Mainz, 1969), pp. 315–333.

however, in the form of soliloquy interpolations—the remembrances, dreams, and visions of the characters. In these visionary islands we glimpse the unfolding of a long-range cosmic process of a scope beyond human comprehension. This is taken as the background against which the events of the particular period are to be understood. In these cosmic visions, however, time actually ceases to be important, and it is really the world of the unconscious and its archetypes that we are entering. Hebbel seems quite serious about the ultimate validity of visionary imagination; he believes that fantasy dips from that wellspring from which the world itself issued forth.[26] In such passages he seems to have reference to a definite type of mental experience, probably of a spontaneous psychedelic nature.

Through the use of these cosmic visions, Hebbel gives the mythical motifs a power, urgency, and vividness which they lack in the twelfth-century version. As is only fitting, he draws more heavily in these passages upon the more vital mythical tradition of the Norse sources.

In order to discover the meaning of the main mythical motifs for Hebbel—the Nibelungen treasure, the Siegfried-Brunhild relationship—it is necessary to examine these visionary passages in some detail. Not only Brunhild, but her nurse, Frigga, Dietrich, the fiddler, Volker, and, to a lesser extent, Hagen, claim to have intimate knowledge of the workings of the cosmos, while Siegfried's memories extend into the legendary world of treasure, dragon, and fire-mountain; and in all of these cases the author's fantasy evidently plays a larger role than Norse or other sources. There is a certain amount of contradiction among the examples. It is clear that Brunhild, with the help of Frigga and Odin, has, through a quickened understanding of the music of the spheres, become aware of her role as a changeling substituted for the dead child of a dead queen, a

[26] "Daß die Phantasie aus derselben Tiefe schöpft, aus der die Welt selbst . . . hervor gestiegen ist" (*Briefe* VII, 302–304).

divine child who will rule death-free over the world (*Siegfrieds Tod* [Siegfried's Death], act I, scenes 1 and 2; act III, scene 7). It is Siegfried's role in this which is ambiguous. At times it resembles the role of the male black widow spider: Hagen cynically remarks that Siegfried, having slain the dragon, must share its fate (lines 2171–2172), and Frigga believes that Brunhild can still be victorious over Siegfried if, while loving him, she still does battle with him (line 932).

Hagen also realizes, however, that Brunhild is driven by an insensate urge to unite with Siegfried to perpetuate a superhuman race. This is confirmed by a passage cut by Hebbel for theatrical purposes and never restored. Here Dietrich says that the world is in a state of millennial upheaval; Siegfried and Brunhild are to found a new race that will supplant humanity. Humanity, however, feeling itself threatened, is to produce an enticing second bride for Siegfried.[27] Thus, Dietrich's revelations from the water sprites in the published version, his remarks about the last autumn of nature and the new spring to come (lines 3568–3583; 4810–4852), take on a more concrete significance. There are two "scenarios" to the cosmic-mythical plan: Brunhild will win over Siegfried and become an eternal Magna Mater, or she will be conquered by him and breed a new race. Siegfried's inability or unwillingness to show love toward Brunhild and his deviousness in wooing her for another has foiled both plans and has saved humanity, for the time being, from any sort of grandiose alteration.

One may ask why Hebbel deleted this rather impressive bit of mythologizing. Perhaps he felt that the specific details of the cosmic plan detracted from its mystery. Perhaps, too, he felt that he had made the alternative to continuation of the human race too attractive. We seem to touch a troubling spot in Hebbel's world view here: the basic ambiguity of his outlook with regard to historical change. His remarks on the transitions be-

[27] De Boor, pp. 275–276.

tween ages as depicted in his works have been a thorn in the side of Hebbel criticism, since they seem not to fit the situation actually present in the works. He seems to share the view, still widely held in his day, that history represents an upward progression, an evolution of mankind toward greater perfection. It is this view that forms the basis for the more ambitious Romantic attempts at a new mythology. The equivocal framing of some of Hebbel's remarks leads us to wonder, however, whether his confidence that a new age must be better than an old one may be wavering. He seems especially hesitant to apply the concept to his own time. Does his Meister Anton fail to understand the world because of his lack of insight, or because the world is, after all, not comprehensible? This leads us to consider a further possible reason for Hebbel's deletion of the Siegfried-Brunhild passage: his deep fear of the type of historical change that he finds so admirable in past epochs.

In view of the psychohistorical parallel, we may carry this line of thought a step further and conjecture that the change Hebbel fearfully anticipates on the historicocosmic scale is really incipient within himself; in his visionary thinking he is actually on the verge of experiencing a death-and-rebirth fantasy urged upon him by his organism in its need for greater psychic harmony and wholeness. We know that he was early attracted to Gotthilf Heinrich Schubert's transcendental interpretation of insect metamorphosis and was disturbed by threats to this interpretation, which he nevertheless was eventually forced to abandon.[28]

One may conclude from Hebbel's biography that he never attained very great integration. His thinking remained essentially encapsulated in, and identified with, his conscious ego, dominated by intellect or by the "demonic" ego-serving pas-

---

[28] Wolfgang Liepe, "Hebbel zwischen Schubert und Feuerbach," in his *Beiträge zur Literatur- und Geistesgeschichte* (Neumünster, 1963), pp. 158–192, esp. pp. 171–172.

sions, while he remained accessible to tender feeling only at
certain moments; he once wrote to Elise that his soul sat cower-
ing like a child waiting for the storm of passion to subside.[29]

Like Grillparzer, Hebbel rationalized his psychic disparity by
relating it to the dichotomy of contemplation and action and by
invoking the exceptional nature of genius. While Grillparzer, no
doubt under Romantic influence, identifies with the passive-
intuitive artist prototype and casts his more sympathetic characters in this mold also, Hebbel draws upon a different tradition:
the nineteenth-century exhumation of the *Kraftmensch*, the
egoistic genius of action, with which he in turn has an evident
rapport. If Grillparzer is possessed by his anima, Hebbel is
possessed by his shadow.

Authors who are psychically disorganized—Grabbe and C. F.
Meyer come to mind; both are authors whose comments on
their own work, like Wagner's, are highly suspect—tend to
favor the latter prototype, since, having no concept of the Jungian suprapersonal Self, they equate Selfhood with the intellec-
tualized, strong-willed ego and follow this ego, through their
characters, in a fruitless and never-ending quest for the Self,
which they seek to realize in ever more frantic self-assertion
and wearing of masks. In Hebbel's case, one thinks especially of
Holofernes and Herodes.

In his historicocosmic mythologizing, Hebbel may actually

---

[29] "O, es ist oft eine solche Verwirrung in meiner Natur, daß mein
beßres Ich ängstlich und schüchtern zwischen diesen chaotischen Ström-
ungen von Blut und Leidenschaft, die durcheinander stürzen, umher irrt,
der Mund ist dann im Solde der dämonischen Gewalten, die sich zum
Herrn über mich gemacht haben, und ganz bis ins Innerste zurück-
gedrängt, sitzt meine Seele, wie ein Kind, das vor Tränen und Schauder
nicht zu reden vermag und nur stumm die Hände faltet, und erst, wenn
der Sturm sich gelegt hat, wieder zum Vorschein kommt" (Letter of
September 3, 1840, to Elise, cited by Wolfgang Liepe, "Zum Problem der
Schuld bei Hebbel," in *Hebbel in neuer Sicht* [see note 25], p. 44). See
also Kurt Esselbrügge, "Zur Psychologie des Unbewußten in Hebbels
Tagebüchern und Briefen," *Hebbel-Jahrbuch* (1960), p. 119.

be attempting to open the hard shell of demonically driven ego to permit it to blend with emotional and intuitive components. His views on the role of man and woman (as in the poem "Mann und Weib" [Man and Woman]) bear this out. Man realizes the cosmic plan piecemeal in his actions, while woman has a direct intuition of it. In lyric moments and in inspired fantasies, Hebbel takes over the woman's role (he is momentarily possessed by the anima), but he apparently cannot relate this phase to his everyday personality. Herodes and Mariamne form a double protagonist; if they were somehow fused, they would form one sympathetic and efficiently functioning person.

As with Grillparzer, we must admit to the aesthetic validity of portrayals of conflict and stagnation, but, again, we cannot help feeling that Hebbel's production would have been better for some greater degree of psychic integration. On the other hand, the saving grace of seeming modernity in his plays is provided by the feeling conveyed by the characters that they are caught up in some vast process whose significance escapes them.

If Herodes and Mariamne stand as conflicting mental components, perhaps the work, and the world in which they move, can be taken as a depiction of the human mind, specifically that of the author. *Die Nibelungen*, regarded in the same light, presents a disconcerting picture. The hero (the ego) departs early, and his role is usurped by two suspiciously regressive figures: the shadow (Hagen) and the growingly sinister anima (Kriemhild). Representations of the Self appear (Dietrich, Attila), but they are strangely ineffectual and resigned.

Hebbel, of course, inherited much of the psychological symbolism of impaired development from his medieval source: the failure of Siegfried and Brunhild to achieve the destined union, for no very compelling reason; the mythical hero Siegfried's slight degradation, attendant upon his assimilation into a civilized and prosaic milieu; the demeaning death of the hero, not

unmythical but lacking in the appropriate cultic grief; the re-
sunken treasure, which nevertheless continues to have an evil
influence (it is, incidentally, thought to have actual commercial
value here); and the emergence of the sinister anima figure,
Kriemhild, a regressive substitute for the destined mate. Her
revenge, which must have seemed gruelingly drawn out even to
the medieval audience, is understandable, like Medea's, as the
natural form of expression of the archetypal mother.

It is in his personal touches that Hebbel reveals his attitude
toward the material, and he does seem to confirm the significance we have found, though there may be technical dramatic
reasons for the changes, in addition. Thus, he has Siegfried
make a first, uncompleted journey to Brunhild's castle, strength-
ening the mythical tie between them. Brunhild is more mythic
and titanic (Hebbel felt that she intruded even into the medieval version like a partly written hieroglyph);[30] she already
shows in her own person the transition to wicked Earth Mother
carried further in Kriemhild. After Siegfried's death she becomes a vampiric living-dead figure, squatting on his grave and
clawing at her own face. Hagen's shadow nature is stressed
when Hebbel, like Wagner, makes him an elf-child in accordance with the Norse sources. The marriage of Kriemhild and
Attila, though it suggests the alchemists' "marriage of the King
and Queen," a variation on the auspicious union of opposites, is
shifted far toward the sinister region; they exchange "dis-
graceful kisses, between life and death, in the terrible night."[31]
When Kriemhild finally demands the treasure's whereabouts
from Hagen, it is in order to give it to the last surviving,
maimed, Hun soldier, as compensation for the Huns' support.
This may be a favorable sign, if not of rebirth, at least of

[30] "Brunhild, . . . die in das Ganze, wie eine nur halb ausgeschriebene
Hieroglyphe hinein ragt" (*Briefe* V, 349).

[31] ". . . Schauderküsse zwischen Tod und Leben/ Gewechselt in der
fürchterlichen Nacht" (*Werke*, IV, 282).

emergence intact from the fearsome death fantasy. When Dietrich is asked by Attila at the end of the drama to take over the reins of the world, he calls up the image of the crucified Christ, a symbol, to be sure, of rebirth, but also the embodiment of the defeated and mutilated hero reclaimed by the Mother.[32]

It is in the treatment of the treasure that Hebbel, like Grillparzer, shows himself most responsive to the archetypes, though at the same time strangely blind to their true significance. The role of the treasure in the action, rather meager also in the original, has not been measurably changed, but its mythical overtones are considerably enhanced, namely in the vision of Volker (*Kriemhilds Rache* [Kriemhild's Revenge], act IV, scene 1). According to Volker, the treasure was originally black, with only occasional phosphorescence. It was apparently amorphous and lying in the open, underfoot, for it gave off sparks when struck by a horse's hoof. Later it was swallowed up by the earth, to be guarded by dwarfs until Odin and Loke raised it. It began to glow a fiery yellow when a piece of it was used for a murder. The more it glowed, the more it was desired and fought over. The more blood flowed, the more it glowed. It is to reach its full brightness when everyone has been killed off. Hebbel's wording is confusing here, since the gold becomes redder, therefore in a sense darker, with increasing luminosity.[33] As if this were not enough, an explicit curse is laid upon the gold: whoever possesses it will die before he can enjoy it. If it becomes ownerless through excessive murder, the world-fire, Ragnarök, will issue forth from it.

Hebbel, perhaps guided, like Wagner, by bourgeois-rooted antibourgeois scruples about material possession, seems blind to the auspicious side of the treasure's symbolism. His ambiguity as to the treasure's brightness may be a sign that the

[32] See De Boor, pp. 37–58.
[33] "In Strömen rinnt das Blut, und wie's erstarrt,/ Verdunkelt sich das Gold, um das es floß,/ Und strahlt in hellerm Schein" (lines 4309–4311).

favorable side is breaking through, as may the virtual identifi-cation of the treasure with blood. For both fire and blood may be associated with vitality as well as with destruction; the darkening may be a brightening; murder and death may signify a renewed springing forth, suppressed here, but impending in the other visionary contemplations of the cosmic plan.

Hebbel shows that he is well aware of this positive symbol-ism in his diary entries upon seeing his wife play Kriemhild in Raupach's play (the stimulus, it will be remembered, for his own work): "Tine as Chriemhild: a black flame! Magnificent! Overwhelming! . . . Black flame, flame of the Last Judgment! The red flame consumes also, but it has the color of life, for blood is red, and from blood all life stems."[34]

A visionary remark of Brunhild's may, unfortunately, sum up the prospects for vitality and rebirth in Hebbel's world: the king will die before morning, and his son, stifling in the mother's womb, cannot be born (lines 908–910). Hagen, however, in his isolated remarks on the treasure, toward the end of the play, seems to see the brighter side. He speaks of a staff that will raise the dead—though he appears to be joking—and, though he does not reveal the whole secret, he knows that the treasure contains a ring capable of producing more gold at will (lines 4397–4405). The libido, properly channeled and properly tapped, constitutes a virtually endless source of creative energy.

Bearing in mind the psychohistorical parallel and its possible application in Grillparzer's case, we might ponder the broader implications of Hebbel's drama of mismanaged mythic mar-riage, bungled treasure-raising, and catastrophic feminine re-

---

[34] *Tagebücher* III, 265, entry no. 4244 (August 29, [1847]): "Tine als Chriemhild: eine schwarze Flamme! Groß! Übergewaltig!" and the following entry: "Schwarze Flamme, Weltgerichts-Flamme! Die rothe Flamme verzehrt zwar auch, aber sie hat doch die Farbe des Lebens, denn roth ist das Blut und aus dem Blut kommt alles Leben." See also Dieter Gerth, "Die Struktur der reduzierten Individuation bei Friedrich Hebbel," *Hebbel-Jahrbuch* (1968), pp. 9–44.

venge. Perhaps the most striking thing about the medieval *Ni-belungenlied* is its apparent success despite grave structural flaws. Hebbel tries to patch some of them, but he is left with a scarcely less unwieldy work, which we know to have had considerable success. Perhaps both the Hohenstaufen empire and the pre-Bismarck era were in need of a work typifying the struggle toward unity and the struggle to reassimilate the national myth. If so, there is no more reason to be optimistic about imminent rebirth, integration, or the productive channeling of subterranean energies on the national scene than there is with regard to the author's psychic constitution.

In the case of both Grillparzer and Hebbel, we have the example of an ambitiously planned work, intimately bound up with the psychic problems of the author, a work replete with symbols of psychic progress but one in which the integration process is undercut at every step, both within the work and within the author. The result is a "monster" (both authors refer to their works thus), a work in which the content outgrows the form. Both authors grope toward the idea of greater self-realization, and both suffer from a sharp contrast of emotional and intellectual components, and they project this problem into bizarre and sometimes unfruitful man-woman relationships. Both are on the verge of change but cannot take the further step, and both are more enamored of Thanatos than of Eros. Both, however, are symptomatic of their age, an age which feared revolution and tumult and attempted to keep the chicken in the egg, an age which preferred fragmentation to integration and rebirth.

If we apply our findings in turn to Wagner, we are struck by the fact that, for all his insight into depth psychology, he does no more than hint musically at a rebirth after the *Götterdämmerung*. The ring is returned to the Rhine. The immolation of Brünnhilde, mythically necessary but otherwise less than compellingly motivated, is the culmination of a rising tide of pathos which seems unable to work through to a catharsis despite mighty efforts. Thus we may ask whether Wagner's failure to live out some of the psychic transformations symbolically depicted in his works was really without detrimental influence on these works. The age, however, was one that demanded and got monumental symbols of aborted rebirth.

POSTSCRIPT

The following remarks were prompted by the discussion subsequent to the delivery of this paper.

As regards the basic assumption of this paper—that there are identifiable recurring patterns of imagery which are especially evocative of an emotionally charged sense of recognition in a manner not readily explained by surface considerations—the best argument for it is provided by the patent inadequacy of the chief counterargument: that literary effects are produced by craftsmanlike manipulation, that they represent clever rearrangements of things already known and recognized and present in the intellectual climate. It seems to do better justice to the phenomenon to assume that the artist creatively reexperiences—or prefigures—the problems of the age in his own terms and formulates that which had been awaiting formulation in the society at large.

Myth is not synonymous with artistic creativity, but it shares with it the ability to call forth wonder at the appearance of something startlingly old in a startlingly new form. If we attempt to account for the phenomenon at all, we must be prepared to probe depths, not merely to map surfaces.

The intent of this paper is not to claim that the works in question were all singularly successful, either as mythical or as artistic creations. There is ample evidence, however, that they were conceived with the deep psychic involvement that attends all visionary activity, whether or not it turns out to be artistically productive. Thus, they are far from being mere attempts to capitalize on a wave of neoclassicism or of nationalistic fervor, or on a widespread penchant for the monumental; neither are they mere exercises in the adaptation of major classic and archaic themes. Practical exigencies of technique triggered a poetic vision; the vision failed to find its proper channel and its fitting form, thus it was poorly realized. Our aim has been to suggest some reasons, pertaining both to the artists concerned and the milieu in which they found themselves, as to why this strikingly inadequate realization took place. Archetypal symbols of psychic death and rebirth seem to bring us closer to these reasons.

It is our contention, further, that artistic or literary merit necessarily presupposes some degree of psychic involvement, and that, therefore, even overt symbols, such as political ones, may have an archetypal component. This becomes clear when such symbols are investigated in depth, for example, in Jost Hermand's Gotthelf study, "Napoleon und die Schwarze Spinne: ein Hinweis" (*Monatshefte* 54 [1962]: 225–231), the central thesis of which is that the spider is a symbol of creeping liberalism. The point becomes more convincing the less we regard the symbol as overtly didactic and the more we assume that the sociopolitical matter has activated personal archetypes, and that liberalism has become amalgamated, in the recesses of Gotthelf's mind, with more elemental menaces. The vividness of the imagery suggests this, and it seems the more attractive of the two possibilities. Gotthelf's spider is, in fact, one of the most successful specimens of modern mythmaking and should serve as a reminder that the capacity for making and apprehending myths is ever with us.

It was questioned whether the works dealt with were typical of their period. It seems clear that anything which rises to prominence within a period must be typical of it. It is obvious, further, that the question of the historically typical is closely involved with that of immediate popularity (and all of the works discussed were quite well received) but much less closely involved with real creativity or with the inherent aesthetic worth that seems to be implied by long-term recognition. It is claimed that the works are indeed typical, as embodiments of prevailing problems, not, however, that they are exemplary.

As regards the more subtle objection that Grillparzer's *Vließ* and Hebbel's *Nibelungen* stem from such divergent periods as to preclude reference to a general "spirit of the age," one can, at the present stage of literary study, only express an opinion as to where periods and ages should be demarcated. It is my estimation that the German-language literature between 1815 and 1890 shows, on the whole, more coherence of cultural orientation than it shows divergence. There is, to be sure, some justification in regarding 1830 as a significant intellectual watershed, but the claim that 1848 and 1871 left appreciable traces on the literature as momentous turning points remains unconvincing. Further, Grillparzer, in his cultural attitudes, is forward-looking, even prophetic, while Hebbel, though he makes much of historical change, essentially looks backward and remains infatuated with the status quo.

A further objection touches upon basic questions of the psychological approach to literature and thus seems to deserve comment here. It is not the intent of this paper to claim that the quality of a work of art is directly dependent either in a positive or a negative way upon the mental well-being of the artist. To claim that the two things are entirely unrelated, however, is to arrive at too easy a solution for a problem that is both perplexing and fascinating. And while it may not be the primary task of the literary scholar to pursue such connections, it is difficult to see why they should not be pursued at all. To disregard the origins of the work of art is to discard valuable insights into its proper appreciation. Mental crises, whether fortunately or un-fortunately resolved or not resolved at all, unusual adaptations to reality, and unusual channelings of libido that we would re-gard as neurotic in daily life, have all been observed to attend the inception of the creative product more often than coinci-dence would allow, and the wise path would seem to consist in taking them into account without allowing considerations of morbidity or health to affect our estimation of the product in any simplistic way. It is my assumption, however, that an enervating psychic stagnation with perpetual, unresolved conflicts is, in the long run, no more auspicious for aesthetic production than it is for any other kind of production, and that a happy blend of form and content is the product of a mind that, however neu-rotically driven, is "healthy" in the sense that it can make vigor-ous use of available energies.

Much of the symposium discussion revolved about Professor Hermand's apparent view of myth in modern times as a regret-table reversion to primitive modes of thought, an abandonment of reason, an invitation to sinister and cynical manipulation. I would agree that contemporary problems must be approached with a maximum of rational effort, but I would protest, with C. G. Jung, that an overweening rationality which has divorced itself from the unconscious and its archetypes, and which seeks to deny the existence of these archetypes as potent, potentially benign psychic realities, is in itself a highly sinister threat to our survival. Dismissal and denial of unconscious material amounts to suppression of it, and we may be sure that our demons, thus left unconfronted and unrecognized, will soon take possession of our minds in the guise of reason. Even pre-Nazi and Nazi Germany might have benefited from a realistic and respectful assessment of its deeper psychic needs; such an assessment might have forewarned against the spurious at-tempts to cater to those needs. The tragedy of the nation at this juncture was that it relied upon its reason, only to find its reason tainted by a monumental irrationality which it had failed to perceive. Goebbels played on the instincts of his listeners; but, like all demagogues, he also played on their easy belief in the supremacy of their rationality, as he no doubt believed, also dubiously, in the supremacy of his.

For that matter, the credentials of pure rationality as a guardian of humanitarian values have always been dubious. The question is whether, in severing our connections with myth, we do not of necessity sever our connections with compassion.

The Distorted Vision:
Pre-Fascist Mythology
at the Turn of the Century

The University of Wisconsin at Madison
Translated by H. G. Huettich and Gregory Mason

"German Fascism" is, I am sure, a lecture topic of which many of you have long ago grown sick and tired. For decades now, one has heard talks on the "Demon Hitler," the "Mephistophelian Goebbels," the slugger gangs of the SA, the inhumanity of the concentration camps, and the barbaric anti-Semitism of the Brownshirt era. And justly so! Because one cannot be too horrified about an undisputable crime, be it the attempted "Final Solution," the Moscow show trials, or the My-Lai massacre. Decisive in such things is not the intellectual claim to originality, but the individual commitment that is forever challenged anew. Political crimes remain despicable, even when they have been rehashed a hundred times and the merely fashionable *engagé* people are already *dégagé* and on the lookout for a new fad.

Even so, those who have become bored with the permanent

debate about fascism are quite justified on one point. The constant talkathon about national socialism is often extremely monotonous and stereotyped. Again and again the "demonic Hitler" is attacked, in a way which obstructs the exposition of fascism as a precisely definable phenomenon of certain societies in a situation of crisis. Even today, journalists primarily concerned with creating a sensational effect use such terms as "madness," "infection," and "pact with the devil" when they talk about fascism. Instead of coming to terms with the ideological prehistory and the capitalistic background of fascism, they usually approach it in strictly phenomenological terms. An attempt is made to distill fascism from the "essence" of the German people, or from the "soul" of Hitler.

This still leaves the origins of nazism largely in the dark. Repeatedly, the years between 1919 and 1922 are investigated in order to discover the sources of the Hitler ideology.[1] If the precursors of Hitlerism are ever mentioned, the namedropping is generally restricted to the greats. Wagner and Nietzsche, sometimes Chamberlain and Gobineau, and, most recently, even Lagarde and Langbehn are mentioned. More obscure authors are seldom even considered.[2] There is no doubt that these names have something to do with the prehistory of national socialism. But are they really the most important ones? Weren't societies, clubs, fraternities, lodges, and other organizations which were much more obscure, trivial, and sectarian, of even greater importance? I refer to the pre-Fascist jungle existing

[1] See Georg Franz-Willing, *Die Hitlerbewegung. Der Ursprung: 1919–1922* (Hamburg, 1962).
[2] Exceptions are Reginald H. Phelps, "Before Hitler Came: Thule Society and *Germanen Orden*," *Journal of Modern History* 35 (1963): 245–261; George L. Mosse, *The Crisis of German Ideology: Intellectual Origins of the Third Reich* (New York: Grosset & Dunlap, 1965), pp. 13–125; Richard Hamann/Jost Hermand, *Stilkunst um 1900: Deutsche Kunst und Kultur von der Gründerzeit bis zum Expressionismus* (Berlin: Akademie Verlag, 1967), pp. 52–81.

around 1900,[3] the historical exploration of which has progressed rather slowly to date. All this has been neglected, even despite Hitler's *Mein Kampf* (1925), in which he tells about his "Viennese years of learning and suffering" before 1914, and clearly states that he laid the "granite foundation" of his world view during that time. Later, as he states, it was "not necessary to change anything."[4] Who were these shadowy figures and obscure pre-Fascists around 1900? A few of them, including the peculiar Jörg Lanz von Liebenfels, whom Wilfried Daim presented in his sensationalized book *Der Mann, der Hitler die Ideen gab* [The Man Who Gave Hitler His Ideas],[5] have now become known. But many of them are still waiting in the wings for their debut and consequent unmasking. I hope to shed some light on these shadowy regions by focusing on the German mythology which is centrally connected with the rise of national socialism.

There are many reasons why this subject has been avoided until now. Some of them involve conscious attempts to veil the situation in order to obscure the politicoeconomical mechanisms I have already mentioned. Others can be credited to intellectual embarrassment which prevented a clear exposition of the romantic irrationalisms of the German past and the exposure of the philosophical preconditions of fascism. Some of the sacred cows, at least, had to be spared association with nazism. There

---

[3] A good cross section of this pre-fascist jungle is offered in *Was tut not? Ein Führer durch die gesamte Literatur der Deutschbewegung,* ed. Rudolf Rüsten (Leipzig, 1914).

[4] The title of the second chapter: "Wiener Lehr- und Leidensjahre"; "In dieser Zeit bildete sich mir ein Weltbild und eine Weltanschauung, die zum granitenen Fundament meines derzeitigen Handelns wurden. Ich habe zu dem, was ich mir so einst schuf, nur weniges hinzulernen müssen, zu ändern brauchte ich nichts" (Adolf Hitler, *Mein Kampf* [Munich: Verlag Franz Eher Nachfolger, G.m.b.H, 1934], pp. 18, 21).

[5] Wilfried Daim, *Der Mann, der Hitler die Ideen gab: Von den religiösen Verirrungen eines Sektierers zum Rassenwahn des Diktators* (Munich, 1958).

were also many who were simply honestly duped by Hitler's frequent statements that national socialism—despite the passages from *Mein Kampf* like the one just cited—was his own original and highly personal creation which could only be understood as his private myth. As early as 1933, anyone who opposed this authoritarian doctrine was ruthlessly silenced. Many of the old folkish voices of that time were simply prohibited from publishing, in order to eliminate them as rivals. For example, Rudolf von Sebottendorf's book *Bevor Hitler kam*, originally titled *Von Thule bis Hitler*, was seized and banned by the Gestapo in the spring of 1934.[6] The painter Fidus experienced a similar fate: The sale of his Teutonic postcards was prohibited—to prevent anyone from gaining an insight into the obscure prehistory of the Nazi movement.[7]

Today's historian should demonstrate enough farsightedness not to be led astray and caught in the trap of the Hitler mystique. Such problems cannot be faced with any false embarassment or irrationality. If there had been only one type of fascism, Hitler-fascism, as some still profess today, then it could be viewed as an isolated episode. To concern oneself with the myth of a twelve-year regime which can only be explained as the direct and personal result of Hitler is certainly not worth the sweat of critical brows. For fascism becomes interesting only when one considers it in its larger perspective. It must be seen as a maneuver of ideological propaganda in a time of political crisis; a maneuver designed and directed by the rulers using the folkish myth to bring an anxious and restless people under its yoke. In such times the populace is fed heaps of emotionally stimulating clichés, and any rational interpretation of the concrete situation is skillfully diverted. Such ideologies are not

---

[6] See Phelps, "Before Hitler Came," p. 245.

[7] See Jost Hermand, "Meister Fidus: Vom Jugendstil-Hippie zum Germanenschwärmer," in Jost Hermand, *Vom Schein des schönen Lebens*, Studien zur Jahrhundertwende (Frankfurt am Main: Athenäum, 1972).

simply bolts from the blue, but always have highly complicated historical circumstances as well as consequences. Brecht was right when he said, in 1934: "There are people who think that many changed with the breeze in 1933. It is my opinion that the breeze has always blown from that direction." In 1945, at the conclusion of his *Arturo Ui*, the great gangster parade about the Hitlerian mob-leader of Chicago, Brecht stated to his new audience: "All people have conquered him, but / Don't anyone celebrate prematurely— / The womb from which it crawled is still fertile."[8] Politically farsighted, he was not referring only to Germany. Such mythological representations are latently inherent in all societies as the expression of unresolved contradictions. Only a crisis is needed for them to become manifest.

A people with a long national history and relatively democratic governmental processes is naturally not so open to these dangers. But even the concepts of "the American dream" or the French *gloire* could undergo fascist mythicalization, given the right circumstances. And consider how much greater that danger is in societies which have no such national identity. Consider the danger to a people whose geographical and historical situation is such that they have experienced a series of dislocations or forceful eruptions.

Japan in the thirties springs to mind. Rapidly accelerating industrialization suddenly threatened the national identity, and the result was regression to ancient warrior-samurai ideals. Italy, without a centralized power source for centuries, was reenchanted with the concept of a great Roman Empire under Mussolini. Upon what, then, should Germany, this "come-lately" nation, with unestablished boundaries and changing political circumstances, rely for psychological sustenance? There was simply no revered and glorious history. At a time when

---

[8] "Die Völker wurden seiner Herr; jedoch / Daß keiner uns zu früh da triumphiert— / Der Schoß ist fruchtbar noch, aus dem das kroch" (Bertolt Brecht, *Stücke* IX [Berlin, 1958]: 365).

Japan and Italy already possessed highly organized cultures, the Germans were still roaming swamps and dark forests. Such a nebulous Nordic realm was not likely to present an ideological base for a national fantasy which could support an exalted concept of a "great folkish heritage."

Actually, there were only the ancient Germans, the Teutonic tribesmen—and not much, if anything, was known about them. But because of this lack of knowledge, they became an ideal subject for speculation. Where there are no facts, fantasy is rampant. The basis for speculation was mostly the *Germania* of Tacitus. This small work, in which Germanic tribes appear in an unusually positive light, had been intended as a polemic mirror of morality for the decadent Roman society. The roughhewn northerners are characterized as being loyal, healthy, freedom-loving, moral, brave, simple—all the positive qualities of ancient Rome. By their example, Tacitus wanted to reconvert his prosperity-fattened, morality-slackened countrymen to the ancient Roman *virtus* ideology. This work was newly discovered by the Humanists, and, as early as the sixteenth century, we find it being used as fodder for the cannons aimed at the "new Rome" of the Catholic church. Otherwise quite enlightened, anti-Catholic circles used the *Germania* as a model for a national countermyth which appealed even to such notables as Wimpfeling and Celtis.[9] But this interpretation was overshadowed by the baroque universalism of the seventeenth century and by the cosmopolitan rationalism of the eighteenth century, and was somewhat suppressed for the time being.

The real emergence of this myth-manipulation came around 1800, when the old "Roman Empire of German Nationality" was heading toward its demise. During the years of struggle against the French, an anti-Latin patriotism had developed. This nationalistic mood, suspicious of anything un-Germanic,

[9] Klaus von See, *Deutsche Germanen-Ideologie vom Humanismus bis zur Gegenwart* (Frankfurt am Main, 1970), p. 14.

moved logically into the Nordic, Teutonic realm. The first impulse for Nordic enthusiasm emanated from Herder, who stated repeatedly that every nation must have its own mythology, springing organically from the base of its intellectual power and language. Thus, when the political crisis came to a head, such catchwords were misconstrued irrationally by the young Romanticists and misused to form the jargon of a mythology, with an obviously reactionary basis. These Romantic circles suddenly castigated the entire eighteenth century as rationalistic and therefore French and superficial. The notion of "German depth" was established by contrast. The unhappy aftereffects of this process can still be felt today. Consider Friedrich Schlegel's *Über nordische Dichtkunst* [On Nordic Poetry], Jakob Grimm's *Deutsche Mythologie*, or Karl Müllenhoff's *Deutsche Altertumskunde* [German Antiquity]: Wherever we look, we find myth upheld at the expense of rationality in order to combat "Latin influences" with *Germania germanicissima*. It was in these times that *deutsch* was first equated with Germanic, and that ominous discipline, known today as *Germanistik*, was established.

A book which reinforced this trend was Madame de Staël's new "Germania," *De l'Allemagne* (1810–1813). It was structured, much like the work of Tacitus, as an indirect mirror of morality. In this case, the point was to demonstrate those sylvan and backwoods virtues of morality and idealism to the French, who had been taken in by Napoleon. Thus, this era produced a host of young students, *Turner*, and fraternal groups emulating ancient Germans, appearing as neo-Teutons, and cultivating such virtues as an idealistically embellished prudery, flexed muscles, provincialism, and a great drinking capacity—all in the name of their idol, the ultimately primitive Turnvater Jahn. Today it is difficult to believe that these actions were looked upon as politically radical. But the following era, under the shadow of Metternich, was even more reactionary: It did not even condone this romanticized masquerade with its Teutonic pantomimes. The new direction was a simplistic *Biedermeier* spirit which left all political power in the hands of a royal ruler of heavenly mandate.

New fuel for these tribal fires was not found until the *Gründerzeit*, when open demonstration of nationally "German" emotions was finally condoned. The "Germanic" ideal was called upon again as a result of the peculiar consolidation of the Reich, which was not preceded by the development of a popular front toward that goal. Bismarck's state came about, after all, by a coup. It was a political dictum from above which had no genuine forward-looking content. Its ideologies demanded a desperate search for a "national identity," necessarily in the junk heap of historical props. Thus the official Bismarck-cult (*Der Alte vom Sachsenwalde*, the Germanic Roland), like the Wilhelminian-cult which followed, consisted mainly of Teutonic elements. Even the artists and philosophers of the seventies contributed their two cents' worth to the general Germanomania. Jordan's *Nibelunge*, Dahn's *Kampf um Rom* [The Battle for Rome], Wagner's *Ring des Nibelungen*, Nietzsche's characterization of the "wandering blond beast of the great migrations," and Lagarde's *Deutsche Schriften*, with its Germanicized view of Christianity, can all be understood only by considering the underlying spirit of these years. Wherever one casts his eye, there are anti-Latin posturings, directed, not only against Paris, but, as representative of the dynamic idea of cultural confrontation, also against Rome. The Nordic mania was in full swing. It is no wonder, then, that Kleist's *Hermannsschlacht* was one of the best-loved dramas of the era.

At first glance, it is possible to attribute these developments to the elevated emotional pitch of a "come-lately" nation. These chauvinistic manifestations are by-products of the joy of victory. But, unfortunately, these trends are not restricted to the *Gründerzeit* but increase in vehemence and scope from year to

year. Despite bourgeois intellectual escapades into Impression-
ism and Symbolism and a few brave protests from the young
Naturalists, the Germanic tide rises in the eighties and nineties,
till it becomes a veritable deluge of the most diverse groups,
parties, fraternities, and lodges. In all this, however, it is noticeable that the politically immature bourgeoisie has become
intoxicated with Teutonism. This results in its acceptance of a
spiritual imperialism quite out of keeping with the normal pro-
priety of the German middle classes. The groups include the
Reichshammerbund, the Germanenorden, the Deutschnatio-
naler Handlungsgehilfenverband, the Volkserzieherbund, the
Mittgart-Bund, the St. Georgs-Bund, the Werdandi Bund, the
Deutscher Flottenverein, the Wehrkraftverein, the Wälsungen-
orden, the Skaldenorden, the Deutschsoziale Partei, the Thule
Gesellschaft, the Guido von List Gesellschaft, the Nordungen,
and the Wandervogel, to name just a few. In all of these groups
the Teutonic warrior becomes the dream-fulfillment figure for
the frustrated Walter Mitty Spießbürger. The members surround themselves with Germanic emblems, preferably the swastika, dance around Midsummer Night bonfires, and hold Old
Nordic-style *Thing*-Convocations. Many of them call themselves neo-Romantics, in order to stress their connection with
Romanticism. By doing this, they equate their peculiar campaign against the materialism of the late nineteenth century
with the struggle of the Romantic movement against the rationalism of the eighteenth century. But, viewed critically, the only
thing it has in common with Romanticism is the name. In
reality, this Germanomania is the ideological foundation of a
Reich-concept with explicitly imperialistic intentions. While the
Teutonophiles around 1800 still based their views on the Ro-
mantic-utopian conception of a unified German nation of the
future, the tribal metaphor is now raised to the great sustaining
image of a Nordic elitism in the battle for the well-known
"place in the sun." In domestic politics it is consciously misused

as a "chosen people" myth, instrumental in the defense against the *"Tschandala* ideology" of socialism.

Sociologically, we can extrapolate the following trends. Among the nobility, Count Gobineau was usually taken as the authority. Gobineau divided the central Europeans into three groups: nobility, the pure race; bourgeoisie, the mixed race; and proletariat, the low race. Operating along the same lines, we find Guido von List. In his book *Die Armanenschaft der Ario-Germanen* [Armanism of the Aryo-Germans] (1908), he attempts to trace German nobility back to an ancient Germanic *Armanenbund*, a power-oriented and power-conscious clan which can only live happily under a Nordic *Führer-Kaiser*. The *Tschandala* race of the proletarians appears here as a subjugated brute herd whose only desire is to follow orders.[10] Thus List, like his noble and wealthy sponsors, strongly favored an aggressive imperialism that would open new settlements for the German people. At the same time, the objective was to rid the Reich of the subhuman instincts of the plebeians, diseased by social democracy.

The same holds true for Houston Stewart Chamberlain, whose ideas are also founded on a nobility concept. In his *Grundlagen des 19. Jahrhunderts* [Foundations of the 19th Century] (1899), he substitutes an irrational nobility of blood for the feudal nobility of Gobineau. At the same time, he openly propounds an undisguised imperialism. Chamberlain sees everything, from history, religion, and culture to the creation of nations, as the result of Aryan endeavor. For all other races he simply postulates a complete lack of culture, resulting from a chaotic leveling in the mixture of races. This racist doctrine fosters the ideology that the Germans, the last branch of the Aryan line, have a manifest destiny to rule the world, as well as to protect the human race from complete bastardization. Wil-

[10] Guido von List, *Die Armanenschaft der Ario-Germanen* (Leipzig, 1908), II, 36, 83.

helm II sensed the usefulness of these ideas in the implementation of his "neuer Kurs." In a letter dated December 31, 1901, he refers to Chamberlain as a brother-in-arms of Germania in the battle against Rome and Jerusalem.

This nobility-racism is integrally related to the propaganda of the *Alldeutschen*, including Joseph Ludwig Reimer, Ludwig Kuhlenbeck, Ernst Hasse, and Heinrich Claß. At first they also represented the interests of the landed gentry, but, in the pattern of List and Chamberlain, their emphasis changed, and they became supporters of the captains of industry. They demanded a German *Stammesreich* in which all peoples of Germanic blood, including the Austrians, the Dutch, the Swiss, and the Scandinavians, would be put under a supreme German rule. After 1900, however, there was talk in these circles of a "Pan-Germanic Empire of German Nation," an "all-Teutonic *Civitas germanica*."[11] This illusory realm was to engage in a militant eastward colonization to satisfy the Nordic instinct for imperialism and to open new spaces for settlement.

A related development in this vein was Social Darwinism. Derived from the sociology of the nineties, this was quickly remodeled into reactionary racism. Instead of the sociological division into "classes," the jargon was now simply changed to "races." These myth-manipulators saw the political action of the "races" as determinable by specific primeval instincts. Whether we cite the *Politische Geographie* (1897) of Friedrich Ratzel, or the *Politische Anthropologie* (1903) of Ludwig Woltmann, the patterns are identical. The Social Darwinists recast Nietzsche's anger at the "many too many" into hate for social democracy and the gruesome image of the "age of the masses" constructed by LeBon into an explicit defense of the bourgeois power structure. Even Bismarck's civil laws were regarded with suspicion as "radical pollutants," since they always helped those

[11] Joseph Ludwig Reimer, *Ein pangermanisches Deutschland* (Berlin, 1905), p. 345.

of low racial quality—those who should naturally die out—back to their feet. In opposition, they cite capitalism as the ideal breeding factor because it unmercifully casts out the weak and reinforces the racially pure. The Social Darwinists of the era, then, with the rest of the abundant Germanomaniacs, reached the conclusion that established the Aryans, in their eyes, as the "master race" of the entire species. By this process they exposed their own primitive slaveowner mentality and exposed its basic imperialistic ingredients.

Besides such definable groups as the feudal agrarians, with their Germanic *Junker*-consciousness, the wealthy followers of Chamberlain, the *Alldeutschen,* and the Social Darwinists, there were other forces at work. There were, at this time, an outstandingly large number of middle-class loners and outsiders who also supported the Aryan racial concept and, consequently, the idea of Germanic world domination. The direction of their view was, however, explicitly intellectual and oriented along the lines of an aristocracy of the mind. Hermann Burte, Franz Haiser, and Hans Blüher, who tried to derive their aristocratic position as chosen people from a Nordic-idealistic spiritualism of the soul, come to mind. Others among these spiritualistic Germanophiles relied greatly on their mystical "knowledge" of the "primeval Germanic" past. In this vein, Georg Hauerstein, in his book *Die Sippensiedlung* [The Clan Settlement], urges the reestablishment of old Aryan families, leading to the formation of a *Landkultur* [agrarian culture], which would be based upon the practice of Germanic religion (*Wihinei*), Germanic law (*Ararita*), and Germanic science (*Armanrita*). Similar ideas were brought forth by Philipp Stauff in his study *Runenhäuser* [Rune Houses] (1904). In Rattlar, Wilhelm Schwaner, the author of the *Germanenbibel* [Germanic Bible] (1904) and director of the Volkserzieherbund, built a Teutonic meeting hall complete with open fireplaces, benches, and an Odin-altar. Here

gatherings were held *Unterm Hakenkreuz* [Under the Swas-
tika] (as his book of 1913 was called), where the faithful could
revel in Christo-Teutonic festivals. In Thale, Ernst Wachler, a
member of the Guido von List Society, used the Harz Berg-
theater to hold sentimentalized Edda-evenings, also centered
around an Odin-altar. In his book of 1902, *Asgart und Mittgart,*
Friedrich Fischbach maintained that Homer's *Odyssey* was
really a Teutonic myth and took place on the Rhine. Later,
Ernst Krause and Hermann Wirth revived this idea, with some
modifications.

The same theory of the chosen "master race" runs through
Willibald Hentschel's book, *Varuna: Eine Welt- und Ge-
schichtsbetrachtung vom Standpunkt des Ariers* [Varuna: A
Historical and World View from the Position of the Aryan].
Hentschel, who also founded the Mittgart-Bund, tries to estab-
lish that the demand for a Germanic *Stammesreich* derives from
the primeval Aryan "law of ascending and descending life."
His political ideal was an "agrarian robber-state," led by a Germanic Lycurgus, harking back to the *Rita*-like times of the ancient Nordic people.

The most peculiar manifestation of this "aristocratic" racist
fantasy can be found in the writings of Adolf Lanz, or Jörg Lanz
von Liebenfels, as he called himself from time to time. In 1905
Lanz published the periodical *Ostara*, which at times reached
a circulation of 100,000 copies. It was subtitled *Bücherei der
Blonden und Mannesrechtler* [Library for the Blond and Male
Supremacist]. In the manner of the Social Darwinists, he divides all of humanity into two races: the Aesir, the "Nordic
Gods of the Light," including all blond hero-types, and the
Vanir, the "creatures of the darkness," including *Tschandalas,*
dark-haired runts, and apelike perverts who try to cloak their
inherent inferiority in a pious and otherworldly phraseology.
Instead of succumbing to the ever-increasing tyranny of these

racially inferior hordes, Lanz demands that all those of true Nordic stock unite in a militant fraternity and resubjugate these apemen to the yoke of physical labor.

There is, of course, a multitude of other Germanophiles, run-of-the-mill Aryans, and garden-variety Teutons, besides these aristocratic spiritual elitists. Mostly middle or lower class, they try to compensate for their own shortcomings with feelings of racial superiority. These scourgers of the Socialists, like Adolf Bartels, Albrecht Wirth, and Max Gerstenhauer, who interpreted and condemned every enlightened position as an anti-German plot, belong to this category. Such tendencies become embarrassingly preposterous when they are wedded with theosophical or Aryosophical elements, and the Teutonic is defined in the realm of the occult as a magical pneuma or a charismatic "electron of the gods." This definition was quite influential with the members of the Werdandi Bund, the hammer people, the Schönerer party, the Deutschbund, and Popert's "Vortrupp," which were partly under the unholy influence of Helen Blavatsky and her German disciple Franz Hartmann. It is a curious picture: A generation in starched collars poses as Teutonic warriors. They succumb to the idea that they are eternally circling the Nordic light of the human soul, and that by doing this they can rise above those "many too many" who must flounder in the mud of materialism. If we look closely, however, we see that their goals are by no means so very ethereal, but consistently imply an ideological support of imperialism and an unyielding defense of the bourgeois order against the advancing proletariat.

The process is similar to the technique used later by the Nazis. These private egocentricities are usually packaged in an irrational mythical wrapping. It is not money which is central here, but the blood-imagery. The move into the biologically folkish realm necessitated the attribution of a certain racial quality to the working class as belonging to the mythical Aryan folk community. Thus it was not the working class, but increasingly the Jews, who became the scapegoats on whom all social crises and contradictions could be blamed.

Consequently, around 1900, the stereotype of the Jew was transformed from the Veitel-Itzig type à la Gustav Freytag into a lecherous, bloodthirsty horror-figure with explicit subhuman traits. Suddenly, all the adverse conditions of the time, the dehumanizing leveling process of the city, the increasing de-Germanization, and the cultural decay were the fault of the Jews. Furthermore, the Jews were suspected of forming an international conspiracy whose goal was to throw humanity into complete, racially miscegenated chaos. Alfred Rosenberg later developed this suspicion into the ideology of "the Elders of Zion." But in 1900 the main culprits in these suspicions were, above all, the golden international alliance (the Rothschilds), the red international alliance (Marx, Heine, Lassalle, Bernstein, Liebknecht and Rosa Luxemburg), and the gray international alliance (the press of the large cities which had supposedly turned all journalism into scandal sheets).

The idea of thorough bloodcleansing and Aryan upbreeding of the German people is simply the logical consequence of this type of anti-Semitism. The objective was simple; to place the so-called *Tschandala* races and the "mishmash people" under the strict control of the Teutonic upper level of humanity, and, finally, to liquidate them.

Based on these views, there was, around 1900, great support for the establishment of premarital medical examinations, for the prohibition of racially mixed marriages, and for special awards for pure Nordic marriages. This was usually pursued under the aegis of eugenics, or "racial hygiene," which was popularized by Heinrich Driesmans. Operating from the same conceptual base, Guido von List had already propagated a

"pure breed" of all the remaining Aryan-heroic types, thus pre-
senting the human race with another Aryan elite.[12] The same
racial husbandry was also effected by the *Alldeutschen*. Non-
Aryans in their "Germanic Empire of Teutonic Blood" would
have to remain without offspring, as racial policy demanded,
but their erotic needs could be satisfied in officially sanctioned
bordellos. Joseph Ludwig Reimer sarcastically referred to this
as a "painless," even "pleasurable" means of extermination. Naturally, he encouraged the Aryans to breed actively.[13] "From a
man like Goethe," stated Gustav Frenssen a few years later, "we
would demand many children."[14]

Several blueprints were even drawn up for the practical realization of such upbreeding. In 1904 Theodor Fritsch published
his plan for a "German regeneration congregation." In rural
seclusion, this group would concentrate their efforts on the production and development of a new Aryan leadership caste, by
practicing a most natural life style and by following the social
order of the ancient Germans.[15] Similar settlements were proposed by Ernst Wachler in his novel *Osning* (1914). But Lanz
von Liebenfels was even more radical. He threatened to castrate
anyone of low racial quality and procreative intentions. Liebenfels also dreamed of racially pure colonies, and recommended
racial beauty prizes, cloistered females for breeding purposes,
employment of euthanasia, the radical liquidation of all Jews,
and the stud rights of the "hero."

But again it was Willibald Hentschel, the founder of the
"Mittgart-Bund for the Regeneration of the Germanic Race,"
who was responsible for the most preposterous notions. In

---

[12] List, *Armanenschaft*, II, 70.

[13] Reimer, *Ein pangermanisches Deutschland*, p. 155.

[14] "Es wird die Zeit kommen, wo man . . . von einem Mann wie Goethe
viele Kinder fordern wird" (Gustav Frenssen, *Möwen und Mäuse* [Leip-
zig, 1928], p. 248).

[15] Theodor Fritsch, *Neue Wege: Gesammelte Aufsätze* (Leipzig, 1922),
p. 236.

Varuna he proposed rural Aryan colonies whose members would give up all personal possessions, wear only homespun clothes, celebrate all the ancient festivals, and dedicate themselves entirely to the creation of a racially pure posterity. Hentschel hoped that these eugenic hotbeds, each of which would bring together a hundred Aryan-heroic types with a thousand Nordic females, would provide an annual surplus of 100,000 pure Aryans, from which a "new folkish upper stratum" could be formed.[16] He, like the rest of the eugenicists, blamed the fateful "democratization" of modern life during the nineteenth century for the German people's departure from the "high spiritual level."[17] He objected to the developments which gave a "weakling" the same right to procreation as a divinely chosen, duly appointed hero. In opposition to the traditional bourgeois system of monogamy, Hentschel, like Hans Blüher, demanded the procreative "self-sufficiency of the ruling caste." This included not only the traditional *ius primae noctis*, but the absolute control over the bodies of all Nordic blonde and blue-eyed females.[18] In his little book of 1910, *Vom aufsteigenden Leben* [The Ascension of Life], he fantasizes about a "new God" of the race who demands an annunciation of the worldwide Aryan mission of domination. Hentschel calls for all the Teutonic stud-types to gather on *Walburgen* or *Tanzbergen* (dance mountains) and to engage in battles of sexual selection. This was to ensure that all children would have "heroes for fathers."[19] Only then, he theorized, would Odin, the wandering Nordic god, come back to German soil and reward the efforts of the regenerated Aryans with the magical rune of victory.

---

[16] Willibald Hentshel, *Varuna*, 2d ed. (Leipzig, 1907), p. 610.

[17] Ibid., p. 11.

[18] Hans Blüher, *Merkworte für den Freideutschen Stand* (Hamburg, 1919), p. 39.

[19] Hentschel, *Vom aufsteigenden Leben: Ziele der Rassenhygiene* (Leipzig, 1910), p. 27.

A more mythical and religious racial concept is hardly possible.[20] All this points to the later era of Hitler, Himmler, and Rosenberg. Naked imperialism and the suppression of the workers are cloaked in divine visions, conversions, and blessings, as well as in the entire "chosen people" come-on, in order to make a saleable ideological package. No wonder the myth of the divinely chosen people consistently uses grail imagery.[21] Its syncretic qualities and lack of definition make the figure of the grail-seeker a perfect mythical image for this type of misuse. Speaking of this figure around 1900 connoted not only Wolfram's and Wagner's Parsifal figures, but also Dürer's *Knight*, who triumphs over death, the devil, and all other obstacles in the course of his holy "mission." Even Martin Luther, who, in the jargon of the folkish circles, had freed the Nordic people's Aryan spiritualism from Rome and Judea, was seen in this light. These sentiments are evident in such novels as Guido Kolbenheyer's *Montsalvasch* (1912), Hermann Burte's *Wiltfeber* (1912), and Friedrich Lienhard's *Der Spielmann* [The Bard] (1913). The actions center around archetypal Germanic individualists, grail-seekers, and spiritual reformers hot on the trail of their mythical objective, a new *sanctum sanctorum* for the Germanic destiny.

At the turn of the century there was a whole army of authors citing the need for a new, specifically Germanic religion in the face of "Western" materialism. This would rescue a vital part of the folkish cultural life from the evil designs of internationalism.[22] We find the following religious concepts: The "German

---

[20] See Theodore Ziolkowski, "Der Hunger nach dem Mythos: Zur seelischen Gastronomie der Deutschen," in *Die sogenannten Zwanziger Jahre,* ed. Reinhold Grimm and Jost Hermand (Berlin-Zurich: Gehlen, 1970), pp. 185–188.

[21] See Jost Hermand, "Gralsmotive um die Jahrhundertwende," in *Deutsche Vierteljahrsschrift für Literaturwissenschaft und Geistesgeschichte* 36 (1962): 521–543.

[22] See Mosse, *Crisis,* pp. 31–51.

God" (Paul Ernst), the "pure Krist" (Hermann Burte), the "religion of militancy" (Rudolf Binding), the "German Christians" (Wilhelm Schäfer), the "Germanization of Christianity" (Arthur Bonus), the "faith of the Northern realm" (Gustav Frenssen), and the "German savior" (Friedrich Andersen).[23] Even Artur Dinter's ridiculous view that the teachings of Jesus were "a deeply Aryo-Germanic heroic doctrine" and his comparison of Jesus with Siegfried and Parsifal were taken seriously. In one place he states: "The duke savior himself, inflamed by the holiest wrath, carries our black-white-red swastika banner against Judea and Rome."[24] To support such slogans, he published a new translation of the Gospel in which he used the technique of Ludwig Albert's *Urbibel der Ario-Germanen* [Arch-Bible of the Aryo-Germans] (1921), eliminating all the anti-Aryan elements and emphasizing Germanic bravery in battle.

The most peculiar folkish grail-seekers, however, were those authors who managed to unite the Teutonic myth with occult theosophy.[25] It was primarily Aryan *Pranasophie* which led to the most questionable ideological complexes. Here again we find Guido von List at work. He tries to derive Nordic Armanism in a direct line from the esoteric mystical theosophy of Odinism. This connection was designed to show that the characteristics of the Teutonic religion were both aristocratic, and, at the same time, warlike and imperialistic. It was his opinion also that the Teutonic elders got together in secret graillike sects

[23] See Hamann/Hermand, *Stilkunst um 1900,* p. 160.
[24] "Der Herzog Heiland selber, flammend von heiligstem Zorn, trägt uns die schwarz-weiß-rote Hakenkreuzfahne voran gegen Juda und Rom" (Artur Dinter, *Völkisch-Soziales Programm* [Leipzig, 1924], p. 26).
[25] See Joachim Besser, "Der Okkultismus stand Pate," *Archiv der unabhängigen Gesellschaft zur Pflege junger Wissenschaft und Kunst* (1949), pp. 38–50, and "Die Vorgeschichte des Nationalsozialismus im neuen Licht," *Die Pforte* 2 (1950): 763–784; George L. Mosse, "The Mystical Origins of National Socialism," *Journal of the History of Ideas* 22 (1961): 81–96.

and held spiritual séances on their bearskins. Central to this
"spiritualist" activity were the media, the *Heilsrätinnen*, whose
spiritual revelations were accessible only to those in the contemporary Aryosophic "know." A periodical, *Prana*, also op-
erated on this Aryosophic wavelength. "Prana" is the syncretic
intermingling of the Iranian *Ga Llama, nepesch* of Genesis,
Logos of the Gospel, the Paracelsian spiritus vitae, the "water of
life" of Omar Khayyam, and the *élan vital* of turn-of-the-century
vitalism. A further collection of images, ranging from Aryan sun
savior and the Edda to the magical power of the swastika, finally culminates in a Germanic symbol of action which expresses
the all-encompassing power of Aryan sun worship.[26] The same
ideas are prevalent in the St. George Bund, inspired by Fidus.
The Schaffer-Bund acknowledges racial hygiene and a bio-
sophical swastika ideology in an attempt to emulate old-Indian
fertility rites. But even here, the grail remains the prevailing
symbol. In this vein, Hans von Wolzogen, the editor of the
Bayreuther Blätter, sees religious Germanization as being singularly influenced by the Wagnerian Parsifal syndrome. In
1913, the *Werdandi-Jahrbuch* of Heinrich Driesmans puts a
"eugenetic" Christ in a lineup right next to "Siegfried the
sun-hero," and "Parsifal the grail-seeker."[27] Other Teutonic hack
writers simply changed the picture of the protectors of the grail
from knights of a Christian order into the whole of the Nordic
population and equated the blood of Christ with Aryan blood.
This forced modification consequently led to the thesis that the
Aryan grail would regain its glow only when the Aryans had regained their original racial purity. Ernst Wachler's 1901 book,
Über die Zukunft des deutschen Glaubens [On the Future of
the German Faith], contains the fantastic projection of a time

[26] *Prana* 6 (1915): 567.
[27] *Werdandi-Jahrbuch*, 1913, p. 100.

when the "contained strength" of the German people would, in grail-like transfiguration, "inundate the entire globe."[28]

And, again, Lanz von Liebenfels presents us with the brightest and most peculiar insight into the swamps of this modified grail mythology. As the publisher of *Ostara*, he was so revered in folkish circles that List extolled him as the "Armanic Ulfilas of the future." Interestingly enough, he started his career as a member of a monastic order which he left because he didn't like its "Jewish Jesuitism." He founded a Bund of Aryosophic male supremacists, named the "Templar order" (of which Strindberg was a member), basing it on Christian as well as Nordic religious concepts. To give his movement a base, he purchased the Castle Werffenstein on the Danube in 1908. Conscious of his divine purpose, he raised the first swastika flag in order to illustrate the magical power of the Nordic "god-electron." His followers revered him as a latter-day Christ, the second great reformation figure of world history, who could lead the last remaining Aryo-heroes in the final battle for the world. Through this overemphasis on the racial aspects of the order, the accompanying Christian elements were played down. This was especially evident in his vision of the Last Judgment, which moved closer and closer to a fantastic blood bath culminating in the merciless liquidation of all *Tschandala* and mixed races. In his *Theozoology* of 1905, we find the following racist "Lord's Prayer," which sounds like the battle cry for all the light Aesir: "Our Father . . . as Thou livest physically in the flesh, the blood, the brain, and the seed of the better, nobler beings, the godly men, Thy sons: Hallowed be Thy name which is Thy seed . . . Thy kingdom come. Let the god-men be victorious over the ape-men . . . Give us eternal bread. Give us the heavenly grail." As could be expected, the whole thing reaches a grotesque cre-

[28] Ernst Wachler, *Über die Zukunft des deutschen Glaubens* (Berlin, 1901), p. 17.

scendo, an apotheosis of Aryo-German imperialism: "We will keep our sword sharp and our war-lyre tuned for the day we start reconquering the world . . . The globe is a Germanic colony! To each brave German warrior a farm, to each officer a noble estate! . . . Once more across the Alps, once more toward the East and the West on the ancient ancestral warpaths. Order in this quarreling *Udumu*-mob . . .! 'O come, Frauja, O God of love Jesus!' Those are the last words from Thy incomparable Book, the Holy Writ! . . . Lead us ahead, O victorious conqueror of the apes, and redeem us from the dwarfed Sodomites. Thine is the Kingdom and the Power and the Glory for ever and ever. Amen."[29]

It was in pre-1914 Vienna, the "racially threatened" metropolis of a melting-pot nation, as it was called in the folkish jargon, that this imperialistic-grail idea had its center of fanatical followers. Lanz von Liebenfels, Guido von List, and Georg von Schönerer were active here. It is no wonder, then, that Hitler, who spent these years primarily in Vienna, lifted the lion's share of his ideology from these authors. We have already learned of

[29] "Vater unser . . . der du leibhaftig wohnst im Fleische, im Blute, im Gehirn, im Samen der besseren, edleren, schöneren Menschen, deiner Söhne. Geheiligt werde dein Name, das ist dein Same . . . Dein Reich komme. Lass endlich die Gottmenschen über die Affenmenschen siegen . . . Gib uns das ewige Brot. Gib uns den himmlischen Gralsbecher . . . Wir wollen unser Schwert geschliffen und unsere Kriegsleier gestimmt halten, wenns los geht zur Wiedereroberung der Welt . . . Der Erdball war und ist Germaniens Kolonie! Jedem wackeren deutschen Soldaten einen Bauernhof, jedem Offizier ein Rittergut! . . . Noch einmal über die Alpen, noch einmal nach Ost und West auf uralten Väterkriegspfaden und Ordnung gemacht unter der zänkischen Udumubande. . . ! 'Komme Frauja, Liebesgott, Jesus!' Das sind die letzten Wortes deines unvergleichlichen Buches, der hl. Schrift! . . . Zieh uns voraus, sieghafter Affenbezwinger, und erlöse uns von den Sodomsschratten, denn dein ist das Weltreich und die Kraft und die Herrlichkeit in Ewigkeit. Amen." Jörg Lanz von Liebenfels, *Theozoologie oder Die Kunde von dem Sodoms—Äfflingen und dem Götterelektron. Eine Einführung in die älteste und neueste Weltanschauung und eine Rechtfertigung des Fürstentums und des Adels* (Leipzig, 1905), p. 159.

his assessment of this era in *Mein Kampf*. That the "granite foundation" of his world view was established here remains in evidence right through to his final years. Hermann Rauschning, in *Gespräche mit Hitler* [Conversations with Hitler], writes that Hitler liked to think of himself as the "suffering Amfortas," who would only be cured of his wound after he had cleansed the German blood of all racial impurities. The SS appeared to him as "the fraternity of Knights-Templar around the grail of the pure Nordic blood."[30] The idea of Aryosophic elitism, complete with blood mysticism and fascistic spiritual orders, can easily be correlated to the Nazi poetry of Schumann, Baumann, Anacker, and others, who set Hitler up as a new Christ or a new king of the grail. They, too, write of a bloody Last Judgment while the grail starts to grow in the souls of the pure, folkishly initiated bearers of the *Blutleuchte*, the torch of blood. This was a vision which Alfred Schuler had already equated with the era of the "appearing grail" before 1914.[31] This conjures up a world view which shows the Christo-Germanic grail myth at the turn of the century as only one, albeit very important, formative factor contributing to Nazism.

But we can make yet another important discovery. This view into the pre-Fascist ideological jungle around 1900 unmasks the principally regressive nature of all recent attempts to create or re-create myths. By their archaic nature, myths are extremely simplistic. Thus, their effect today is restricted to unenlightened adolescents, anxiety-ridden neurotics, and religious sectarians. In short, the effectiveness of myth is restricted to all those who are not yet able or who refuse to come to terms with the complexities of modern life, and, instead, driven by frustration and fear, take refuge in such explicitly simplistic world views.

[30] Hermann Rauschning, *Gespräche mit Hitler* (New York: Europa Verlag, 1940), p. 216.
[31] Alfred Schuler, *Fragmente und Vorträge aus dem Nachlaß*, ed. Ludwig Klages (Leipzig, 1940), p. 174.

In contrast, utopian ideology, as long as it is based on rationality, always points to the future. By definition, myth remains stuck in brute, irrational psychic frustrations. Myth, then, can only be fought and denied, while a utopian ideal can at least have the constructive force of a corrective. Naturally, it is better to be able to exist without either of these crutches and to proceed in a completely enlightened fashion, basing all spiritual, political, and social judgments on a concrete evaluation of the actual situation at hand. It becomes evident, however, that this process of judgment demands a "theory," and not just simple pragmatism. Let us base this theory on the principles of rational dialectics oriented toward the advancement of humanization in the coexistence of men. Let us not fall prey to the Romantic fetishism of the eternal day before yesterday.

Hesse, Myth, and Reason:
Methodological Prolegomena

BY THEODORE ZIOLKOWSKI

Princeton University

When I was invited to contribute a paper on Hesse to a symposium concerning Myth and Reason, I accepted with alacrity and confidently proposed a topic, assuming that my talk would virtually write itself in the course of an inspired weekend. After all, "everybody knows" what a central role myth plays in such works as *Demian* and *Siddhartha*; and among the many polarities that Hesse bandies about with such seeming casualness in his essays and letters—nature and spirit, male and female, Yin and Yang—I was certain that there must be many examples of Myth and Reason that would bear out all my instant intuitions. Fortunately for me, prudence overcame self-confidence, and I sat down one weekend several months in advance to pen the little essay that was intended to be graceful yet profound, both learned and elegant. A few weeks and many drafts later, I not only had no paper: I was hopelessly confused

and on the point of denying that any paper, elegant or otherwise, could be written on Hesse in the context of Myth and
Reason. Like the farmer in the classic joke, who is consulted for
directions to a certain town, I had come to the sobering conclusion that "you can't get there from here."

When I finally stopped long enough to analyze the problem,
it became clear that the reasons for my dilemma were in large
measure terminological and methodological. If I have included
the process in the product by incorporating into my paper the
stages of my own perplexity, I have done so not out of simple
pedantry or sheer egomania, but in the hope that the record of
my difficulties may save others from similar stumblings in a
treacherous terrain. Few words in intellectual history are more
ambivalent than the monosyllable "myth." In an essay written
in 1955, Claude Lévi-Strauss observed that the anthropological
study of myth had remained, for more than fifty years, "a picture of chaos."[1] Indeed, virtually every responsible discussion
of myth begins with the troublesome problem of definition. Yet,
as Mircea Eliade has remarked, "it would be hard to find a definition of myth that would be acceptable to all scholars and at
the same time intelligible to nonspecialists."[2] However, for all
their disagreement among themselves, most ethnologists seem
to share a basic consensus that distinguishes their primary
understanding of myth from the various secondary definitions
accepted by nonethnologists. Specialists may argue at length as
to whether myth is infrarational or superrational. They may
disagree on the relative merits of literal versus symbolic interpretation. They may debate whether or not all peoples or com-
munities pass historically through a mythopoeic stage. But the

[1] "The Structural Study of Myth," in *Myth: A Symposium*, ed. Thomas
A. Sebeok (1955; rpt. Bloomington, Indiana: Indiana University Press,
Midland Books, 1965), p. 82.
[2] *Myth and Reality*, trans. Willard Trask (1963; rpt. New York: Har-
per & Row, Torchbooks, 1968), p. 5.

entire discussion takes place within the context of a myth which, in Lord Raglan's definition, is "a narrative associated with a rite."[3]

Now, it is perfectly obvious that when we speak of myth in connection with Hesse or Yeats or Goethe—or, indeed, any conscious aesthetic creator—we are not referring to myth in this primary sense. Literary works have, for the most part, precious little to do with ritual—unless it is the ritual of agony that most writers celebrate in the effort of getting their visions down on paper. As literary scholars we deal for the most part, in Lord Raglan's terms, with "those myths which the classical writers abstracted from their religious context and used as a basis for poetry and romance."[4] That is to say, even when we talk about the figures of Greek mythology—or Norse or Celtic or biblical —we are at least one step removed from the ethnologist's primary myth. And some mythologists are far less tolerant than Lord Raglan when they contemplate our work. The folklorist Stith Thompson refers with considerable disdain to "the recent perversions of the word 'myth' which some of the modern literary critics are employing."[5]

We may not be prepared to accept Professor Thompson's characterization of our endeavors as "perversions." Yet it is perfectly clear that, as literary scholars, we customarily exercise the word "myth" in a secondary sense that has little to do with the meaning current in anthropology or history of religions. As a result, no matter how valuable and exciting those primary studies may be, they often have little bearing on the pursuits of literary criticism. For our purposes we can distinguish at least three senses in which the term "myth" is commonly used in modern criticism. In each case the common denominator is structure rather than content or meaning. First, it is frequently

---

[3] "Myth and Ritual," in *Myth: A Symposium*, p. 122.
[4] Ibid., p. 124.
[5] "Myth and Folktales," in *Myth: A Symposium*, p. 170.

employed to describe those literary works, whether ancient or
modern, that are based upon themes or structures derived from
primary myth. In his recent study of "mythic patterns in the
literary classics" Harry Slochower uses the term "mythopoesis"
to distinguish such derivative versions from primary myth. "The
mythopoeic works examined in this study arose when the literal
account of the legend could no longer be accepted."[6] The works
that he considers—from the Book of Job and Greek tragedy
down to Camus's *The Myth of Sisyphus* (1955)—have divorced
the myths upon which they are based from their ritual origins,
treating the story purely as an aesthetic structure. Similarly,
most of the studies listed in Elisabeth Frenzel's useful bibli-
ography of literary themes, *Stoffe der Weltliteratur* (Stuttgart:
Kröner, 1963), take myth in this sense: the aesthetic shapings of
the stories of such figures as Prometheus, Orpheus, or Electra,
far removed from any ritual associations they may once have
had.

A second sense in which myth has become current among
literary scholars is the one popularized by Jungian psychology,
in which the term designates not the narrative originally associated with a specific ritual, but rather certain universal archetypes that are said to emerge from the collective unconscious.
In the criticism stimulated by this view—notably Maud Bod-
kin's *Archetypal Patterns in Poetry* (1934) and Northrop Frye's
Anatomy of Criticism (1957)—the writers are concerned not
with the specific mythological motifs or figures that interest
Slochower and the thematologists, but rather with such general
archetypal patterns as rebirth or apocalypse.

In a third sense, finally, "myth" is used loosely to describe
various modern works in which the vision is so intense that the
work seems to sum up or exemplify some basic human experi-

---

[6] Harry Slochower, *Mythopoesis: Mythic Patterns in the Literary Classics* (Detroit: Wayne State University Press, 1970), p. 15.

ence. In this sense, for instance, the term has often been applied
to such figures as Faust or Don Quixote, or to the narratives of
Kafka or Dostoevsky, even though none is based explicitly on
motifs originally associated with a ritual or on universal archetypal patterns. Rather, these writers are frequently said to have
created new myths themselves. Notably, within recent years,
students of English literature, for instance, have been increasingly obsessed by what they call the "mythmaking" of Blake or
Shelley or Wordsworth.

Now of all the "perversions" through which we critics are
accused of doing violence to the concept of myth, this third one
is the most objectionable in the eyes of many scholars. Stanley
Edgar Hyman has stated, for instance, that "what such modern
writers as Melville or Kafka create is not myth but an individual
fantasy expressing a symbolic action."[7] To call these fantasies
myths, he argues, is to misunderstand wholly the nature of
primary myth. "No one, not even Melville, can invent myths or
write folk literature." In general, it would probably be better
for everyone involved if we did not try to make the word "myth"
bear almost more meanings than it can sustain. Clearly, in criticism, we all too often use the label "mythic," hoping thereby to
gain an added dimension of allusive profundity, when in fact
we mean mythological, archetypal, or simply creatively imaginative!

Yet for better or for worse, the word has the sanction of usage
in all three of these meanings. And all three senses have been
employed usefully, I think, to characterize certain aspects of
Hesse's writing. In my own studies I have found it fruitful to
investigate to what extent Hesse has consciously exploited patterns and motifs associated with Jesus or Buddha in order to
lend "mythic" structure and meaning to such characters as

[7] "The Ritual View of Myth and the Mythic," in *Myth: A Symposium*,
p. 151.

Demian and Siddhartha.[8] Other scholars—most recently G. W.
Field in his book on Hesse—have devoted particular attention
to the impact of Jung's thought on Hesse, analyzing the archetypal images that play a role in *Demian* and other works around
1920.[9] And, in one of the earliest, and still finest, general essays
on Hesse's works, Oskar Seidlin has argued that Hesse's stories
are "modern myths" because "his entire work seems an endless
recording of the process of awakening."[10] By analogy, many
critics have called *Das Glasperlenspiel* [The Glass Bead Game]
"mythic" because it exemplifies symbolically an important vision of twentieth-century culture. And to move from the sublime
to the ridiculous: it is probably not far-fetched to suggest that it
is the pronounced structural pattern, which in the critical sense
might be called "mythic," that has made *Siddhartha* such an apt
object for parody. I refer specifically to Roger Angell's delightful parody that appeared in *The New Yorker* (March 14, 1970)
under the title "Sad Arthur"; and to the "classy comics illustrated" version published recently in the humor magazine
National Lampoon (February, 1971). As we noted, it is a characteristic of myth in the literary sense that it provides a basic
pattern that can be endlessly repeated and adapted to the
exigencies of each new generation—either seriously or paro-
distically.

To summarize: Literary criticism uses the term "myth" in at
least three ways that are unacceptable to the more rigorous
understanding of ethnology. All objections of terminology aside,
however, these three approaches have produced valuable insights in the study of literary works generally and of Hesse's

[8] Theodore Ziolkowski, *The Novels of Hermann Hesse* (Princeton, N.J.: Princeton University Press, 1965), pp. 118–145 and 151–157.

[9] George Wallis Field, *Hermann Hesse* (New York: Twayne, 1970), pp. 46–56. See also Malte Dahrendorf, "Hermann Hesse's *Demian* and C. G. Jung," *Germanisch-Romanische Monatsschrift* 39 (1958): 81–87.

[10] Oskar Seidlin, "Hermann Hesse: The Exorcism of the Demon," *Symposium* 4 (1950): 325–348.

novels in particular. But if we now consider the specific topic
of this symposium, it turns out that even these definitions current in literary criticism are not strictly germane. For we have
been asked to deal with the subject of Myth and Reason in German literature. But a curious thing happens to the word "myth"
when it is juxtaposed with the notion of "reason": It takes on
still another meaning that is only tenuously related to the primary definition of ethnology and the secondary senses of
criticism.

Inherently there is nothing mutually exclusive about the two
concepts. The classical philologist Bruno Snell claims that the
opposition of *Mythos* and *Logos* is altogether inappropriate,
since myth adumbrates the subject matter of thought while
reason refers to its form.[11] Cultural anthropologists from Frazer
and Malinowski to the present have repeatedly discovered that
myth and reason coexist comfortably among primitive tribes, for
whom myth represents no more and no less than the symbolic
counterpart of abstract rational thought. Similarly, such psy-
chologists and philosophers as Freud and Ernst Cassirer have
argued that there is nothing in the human mind or character to
make myth and reason incompatible.

Yet intellectual history shows us, in contrast, that the notion
of "myth," as soon as it is taken in conjunction with "reason,"
rapidly loses the more or less neutral meaning that it has in ethnology and in literary criticism and becomes the bearer of strong
positive or negative values that have accrued to it in the past
century and a half. In short: in the realm of cultural history the
monosyllable is made to bear yet another set of associations that
have almost nothing to do with the reasonably objective meanings it has developed in other disciplines. Here it is not so much
a descriptive criterion as, rather, a vaguely defined force or
power.

[11] Bruno Snell, *Die Entdeckung des Geistes* (Hamburg, 1948), p. 214.

In German history the word *Mythos* has emerged most conspicuously during periods of irrationalism as an ideal held up
against sterile, destructive rationalism.[12] The obsession with
myth first showed up during the Romantic era when, in a reaction against the Enlightenment, such thinkers as Gotthilf
Heinrich Schubert, Friedrich Creuzer, Joseph Görres, and many
others began their researches into what they called, somewhat
indiscriminately, either myth or mythology. Friedrich Wilhelm
Schelling even intended to write what he tentatively entitled a
"Mythology of Reason."[13] This wave of Romantic interest was
intensified when Wagner and Nietzsche appropriated the term
"myth" to designate the almost organic substance that was supposed to revitalize the enervated culture of Germany. (Charac-
teristically, both men use gastronomic images when they talk
about myth, referring to it as though it were some macrobiotic
diet of the spirit.)[14] Nietzsche praises Wagner specifically because his work is mythic rather than rational. "Wagner's
poetic quality manifests itself in the fact that he thinks in visible and tangible actions, not in concepts—that is to say, he
thinks mythically, just as the common people have always
thought."[15] But it was notably during the twenties and thirties

[12] See Gerhard Schmidt-Henkel, *Mythos und Dichtung: Zur Begriffs-
und Stilgeschichte der deutschen Literatur im neunzehnten und zwanzigsten Jahrhundert* (Bad Homburg-Berlin-Zurich: Gehlen, 1967), pp.
245–277.

[13] Schelling, of course, did write a *Philosophie der Mythologie* (1842).
For the phrase "Mythologie der Vernunft," see Karl S. Guthke, *Die Mythologie der entgötterten Welt: Ein literarisches Thema von der Aufklärung
bis zur Gegenwart* (Göttingen: Vandenhoeck & Ruprecht, 1971), p. 20.

[14] I have attempted to sketch this history in my article "Der Hunger
nach dem Mythos: Zur seelischen Gastronomie der Deutschen," in *Die
sogenannten Zwanziger Jahre*, ed. Reinhold Grimm and Jost Hermand
(Bad Homburg-Berlin-Zurich: Gehlen, 1970), pp. 169–201. The present
piece is in many senses an elaboration of certain implications contained in
that article.

[15] "Richard Wagner in Bayreuth," *Werke in drei Bänden*, ed. Karl
Schlechta (Munich: Hanser, 1954), I, 413.

of this century that myth began to take on the meaning that it still enjoys in the latest edition of the standard dictionary *Sprach-Brockhaus*: a "bildhafte lebenerneuernde Idee"—that is, a life-restoring idea capable of being expressed in symbolic form, as opposed to rational analysis that deals with abstract concepts. For instance, in the introduction to his influential study of Nietzsche, Ernst Bertram remarked that "reason, alert and zealously watchful, erects its immovable barriers today, no less than formerly, wherever a myth attempts to make its way."[16] Similarly, in a study of Schelling entitled *Die Rückkehr zum Mythos* [The Return to Myth], the philosopher Gerbrand Dekker argued that myth, as the "dynamic basis" of our lives, overcomes the highest principle of logic and takes over the guidance of our consciousness.[17] It will be noted that in none of these cases does the term "myth" have the more specific senses that it enjoys in the disciplines of ethnology or criticism: it is neither a narrative associated with a ritual, nor a mythological story, nor a universal archetype, nor an intense poetic vision. Rather, myth is presented as an autonomous life-giving force with no fixed structure or form—a force that exists almost wholly in opposition to a sterile rationality inimical to life.

The most radical extreme reached by the antirational veneration of myth is that compendium of horror that Alfred Rosenberg published in 1930 under the title *Der Mythus des 20. Jahrhunderts* [The Myth of the 20th Century]. In the name of a new unity of body and soul, modern man must escape "a terrible,

[16] Ernst Bertram, *Nietzsche: Versuch einer Mythologie* (1918; 7th ed. Berlin: Bondi, 1929), p. 11.

[17] Gerbrand Dekker, *Die Rückwendung zum Mythos: Schellings letzte Wandlung* (Munich-Berlin: Oldenbourg, 1930), p. 203: "Der Mythos ist, als dynamische Grundlage unseres Lebens, die in daemonischer Vielheit hervorbrechende Potenz. Diese Potenz soll 'im Grunde' bleiben, überwältigt jedoch in der 'Mythologie' das höchste logische Prinzip und bemächtigt sich der Führung im Bewußtsein."

barren rationalism that threatens to choke our soul."[18] The "organic" philosophy of the twentieth century "extricates itself from the tyranny of rational systems."[19] Despite the ravages perpetrated under the aegis of Rosenberg's textbook on the theory and practice of totalitarianism, the old conception of myth as an antirational life-giving power still lives on in the contemporary German language. In his book *Mythos und Logik im 20. Jahrhundert* [Myth and Logic in the 20th Century] Michael Hochgesang maintains that mankind is entering a "new mythic age" which will restore to reality the wholeness that it lost when intellect emancipated itself from myth, thereby creating a blind, sterile, "myth-less" nature.[20] Hochgesang's basic theme is no more modern than Rousseau or Romanticism; but it is characteristic of our times that he has chosen the terms "Myth" and "Reason" to bear the burden of his meaning. Similarly, in a series of lectures on the telling topic *Die Wirklichkeit des Mythos* [The Reality of Myth] sponsored in 1965 by Radio Bavaria, it becomes quite evident that almost all the contributors—including representatives from various intellectual disciplines—regard "myth" in this older sense as a cultural force of considerable power, an organic food required to offset the low-protein diet of mere reason or logic or rationality.[21]

If the term "myth" has often been invoked by antirationalists as a shibboleth of life-giving power, the reverse is no less true. In periods of rationalism—or periods, at any rate, that pride

---

[18] Alfred Rosenberg, *Der Mythus des 20. Jahrhunderts:Eine Wertung der seelisch-geistigen Gestaltenkämpfe unserer Zeit* (1930; rpt. Munich: Hoheneichen-Verlag, 1934), p. 136.

[19] Ibid., p. 697.

[20] Michael Hochgesang, *Mythos und Logik im 20. Jahrhundert: Eine Auseinandersetzung mit der neuen Naturwissenschaft, Literatur, Kunst und Philosophie* (Munich: C. H. Beck, 1965), pp. 41–89.

[21] *Die Wirklichkeit des Mythos: Zehn Vorträge*, ed. Kurt Hoffmann (Munich und Zurich, 1965).

themselves on their self-proclaimed rationalism—myth is made
to serve as a term of opprobrium. Thus Friedrich Theodor Vischer, in sharp contrast to his more Romantically oriented contemporaries, argued, as early as 1848, that "a widespread myth
always comes to its end first in the heads of a minority of men
who think more clearly than the masses."[22] Now rationality and
irrationality have presumably been distributed in equal proportions among the people of the world. If we observe that in German this sense of myth as a "lie" has been largely displaced by
the Romantic understanding of myth as a life-giving power, then
the observation is purely semantic. In the United States, for example, we have discovered other channels for our irrationalism:
one of its names is Indochina. However, in English, as in most
other European languages, the word "myth" has died out in its
positive sense and occurs almost exclusively as a negative counterpart to reason. In French, for example, the word *mythomane*
is a common expression for a compulsive liar. And we need go
no farther than the *New York Times* or any recent bestseller list
to prove a similar point for current American usage. Lewis
Mumford has attacked what he calls the "irrational obsession"
with modern technics in a two-volume work entitled *The Myth
of the Machine*, in which myth is defined disparagingly as a
"disreputable anthropological fable."[23] Victor C. Ferkiss's study,
Technological Man (New York: Braziller, 1969), which won a
National Book Award for 1970, bears the telling subtitle, "The
Myth and the Reality." A bestselling critique of corporate capitalism is called simply *Up Against the American Myth*[24]—and,

[22] *Kritische Gänge*, ed. Robert Vischer, 2d ed. (Berlin and Vienna:
1920), III, 34.
[23] Lewis Mumford, *The Myth of the Machine: The Pentagon of Power*
(New York: Harcourt, Brace, Jovanovich, 1970), p. 209.
[24] *Up Against the American Myth: A Radical Critique of Corporate
Capitalism Based on the Controversial Harvard College Course, Social
Relations*, ed. Tom Christoffel, David Finkelhorn, and Dan Gilbarg (New
York: Holt, Rinehart, and Winston, 1970).

in general, "myth" is an important epithet in New Left rhetoric. Finally, *Time* magazine recently (March 15, 1971) featured a cover-story on "Suburbia: A Myth Challenged." Now in all these cases the usage is revealing: myth is characterized as irrational, unrealistic, disreputable; it is no more than a false belief, injurious to society, that must be challenged by any rational person.[25] The psychotherapist Rollo May attains the ironic inversion of this meaning, in his widely read book, *Love and Will* (New York: Norton, 1969), when he suggests that "rationality" itself is no more than one of our contemporary "myths."

At this point someone might well object that the preceding examples are irrelevant, taken as they are from popular works where usage is not expected to be so precise as it is among scholars. At least two responses would be in order. First, as I hope to show later, popular usage is so strong that it establishes patterns of thought into which even word-conscious literary critics can unwittingly fall. Second, in cultural history meaning is defined by usage; and my topic, as it is gradually emerging, turns out to be an exercise in cultural history. In ethnology, as we noted, the concept of reason is regarded as complementary to myth. In literary criticism the three principal meanings of "myth" simply do not evoke the notion of reason: myth, being basically structural, is neither rational nor irrational. But in cultural history, as we have seen, the terms are anything but objective extrinsic criteria: they have become highly charged vocables, words loaded with subjective associations that vary from person to person, from language to language. The problem as I finally understand it, then, is to determine Hesse's position in the cultural debate on Myth and Reason. We do not inquire,

---

[25] It is symptomatic that the German language, to achieve this negative meaning with no ambiguity, must resort to phrases that qualify the noun: for example, the title of the recent anthology, *Trivialmythen*, ed. Renate Matthaei (März-Verlag, 1971).

from the extrinsic standpoint of criticism, what "mythic" patterns show up in his work; we try not to impose our own understanding of myth and reason on Hesse; we ask simply how he himself understood the concepts Myth and Reason and whether this understanding helps to cast any light on Hesse's position in the cultural situation of his age.

The word "myth" occupies a prominent place in Hesse's vocabulary from the very beginning. The first sentence of the early novel *Peter Camenzind* (1904) reads: "Im Anfang war der Mythus" [In the beginning was the Myth]. When we examine the meaning of the word, we see instantly that it has the conventional associations attributed to it by two models revered by the young Hesse—Wagner and Nietzsche: myth connotes primal powers of vitality and creativity that are characteristic of primitive peoples and not yet eradicated, in the souls of innocent children, by the hostile forces of civilization. "Just as the great god composed and struggled for expression in the souls of the Indic, Greek, and Germanic peoples, thus [myth] creates anew daily in the soul of every child."[26] Later in the novel this understanding is expanded to embrace a Dionysian power that creates meaning out of the chaos of life: "[wine] transmutes the confusion of life into grand myths and plays the song of creation on a mighty lyre."[27] This Romantic reverence of myth is absolutely appropriate in the novel of the Swiss peasant boy who sets out to become a writer but, increasingly disenchanted with the sterility of urbane and rational civilization, ultimately returns to the primal simplicity of his highland home with its eternal "mythic" patterns of existence.

[26] "Wie der grosse Gott in den Seelen der Inder, Griechen und Germanen dichtete und nach Ausdruck rang, so dichtet [der Mythus] in jedes Kindes Seele täglich wieder" (I, 219). Hesse is cited here and below according to volume and page of the seven volume *Gesammelte Schriften* (Frankfurt am Main: Suhrkamp, 1957).

[27] "[Der Wein] verwandelt die Wirrnis des Lebens in grosse Mythen und spielt auf mächtiger Harfe das Lied der Schöpfung" (I, 278).

But if Hesse began with a conventional Nietzschean conception of myth as some vague ordering force, his understanding changed a decade later as a result of his psychoanalysis and his readings in psychology. For the more sophisticated characters of *Demian* (1919) myth is no longer an undefined irrational impulse, but a projection of the collective unconscious in the form of an image. Thus the theologian Pistorius tells Sinclair, in good Jungian terminology, that Christ is "not a person, but a hero, a myth . . . a gigantic silhouette in which humanity sees itself painted on the wall of eternity."[28] (By analogy, Hesse calls *The Brothers Karamazov* a "mythic novel"—not because it represents some inchoate force, but because it exemplifies a "dream of humanity" by means of symbolic or mythic figures [VII, 172].) While Pistorius, the theologically trained analyst, uses the word in a reasonably technical Jungian sense, Sinclair employs the term in a looser, layman's sense to mean no more than "my own profound belief." At one point, for instance, he explains that Demian's thoughts made such a spectacular impression on him because they confirmed his own intuitive notions about the duality of being: "Why, that was precisely my own thought, my own myth."[29]

These few examples are quite representative of Hesse's use of the word "myth" from 1900 to 1920: his usage is wholly conventional—first in the sense legitimized by Wagner and Nietzsche and then in the more specific definition of Jungian analytical psychology. The fact that Hesse used the word with increasing frequency suggests that it was becoming more and more fashionable in the cultural world of the early twentieth century. During the twenties, however, we detect a pronounced change.

---

[28] "Keine Person, sondern ein Heros, ein Mythos . . . , ein ungeheueres Schattenbild, in dem die Menschheit sich selber an die Wand der Ewigkeit gemalt sieht" (III, 204).

[29] "Das war ja genau mein eigener Gedanke, mein eigener Mythus" (III, 157).

The term "myth"—or, frequently, "mythology"—is invoked in an ironic way to designate an individual's idealized and often mistaken notions about himself and the world. In 1924, for instance, Hesse revealed: "I permit myself, with the Madonna, my own cult and my own mythology: in the temple of my piety she takes her place alongside Venus and Krishna."[30] In *Der Kurgast* [At the Spa] (1924), "myth" and "mythology" have been reduced to mean no more than the systematization of subjective beliefs, with no objective validity. "Among cultivated and intelligent people it happens at every moment that each one acknowledges the mentality and language of the other, his dogmatics and mythology, as purely subjective, as a mere attempt, a mere fleeting analogy."[31] And Hesse confides that a faith in the priority of the psychic over the physical belongs to his own "personal biology and mythology."[32] In *Der Steppenwolf* (1927), the term continues to occur in this secularized meaning as a code-sign for the sum of individual—and often mistaken—beliefs. Harry Haller's vision of himself as a dualistic being consisting of *Bürger* and *Steppenwolf*, we read in the Tract, is "nothing but an oversimplifying mythology."[33] Similarly, "All 'explanations,' all psychology, all endeavors to understand require aids, theories, mythologies, lies; and a reputable author should not neglect to resolve these lies, if possible, at the end of his presentation."[34] This clear equation of "mythology" with lies,

[30] "Ich erlaube mir mit der Madonna einen eigenen Kult und eine eigene Mythologie, sie ist im Tempel meiner Frömmigkeit neben der Venus und neben dem Krischna aufgestellt" (III, 896).

[31] "Unter gebildeten und gescheiten Menschen passiert es ja in jedem Augenblick, daß jeder die Mentalität und Sprache, die Dogmatik und Mythologie des andern als eine subjektive, als blossen Versuch, blosses flüchtiges Gleichnis erkennt" (IV, 23).

[32] "Persönliche Biologie und Mythologie" (IV, 24).

[33] "Lediglich eine vereinfachende Mythologie" (IV, 242).

[34] "Alle 'Erklärungen,' alle Psychologie, alle Versuche des Verstehens bedürfen ja der Hilfsmittel, der Theorien, der Mythologien, der Lügen;

bringing us to the opposite extreme from Peter Camenzind's irrational reverence of myth, approaches the jargon of contemporary rhetoric, which uses the word "myth" to designate irrational beliefs that must be eradicated. A similar derogatory conception shows up in a letter of 1939, where Hesse contrasts true religion with false mythology, explaining that "pure religions are for a small group of the elite; the masses require magic and mythology."[35]

It seems clear what is happening here. The word "myth," which Hesse—under the impact of Jungian psychology—was beginning to use with some frequency around 1920, has been contaminated, or at least made problematic, by the political and cultural rhetoric of the twenties and thirties, which culminated in Rosenberg's *Der Mythus des 20. Jahrhunderts.* Just as Hesse, in the thirties, regretfully abandoned the venerable expression *drittes Reich* [third Reich], with its wealth of cultural and religious associations, he now found it impossible to continue to use "myth" in a positive sense, lest it be misunderstood. As a result, he shifted in his public utterances to the term "mythology," which he used in an increasingly disparaging sense to characterize the ideological illusions by which the unthinking mob can be moved. Hesse's new understanding of myth and its inherent dangers has even caused him to look with more skeptical eyes at primitive myths: they no longer have absolute value but only the relative meanings we attribute to them. "The myths of the Bible, like all the myths of mankind, remain worthless for us as long as we do not dare to interpret them personally for ourselves and our times," Hesse wrote in 1930.[36] But, once

---

und ein anständiger Autor sollte es nicht unterlassen, am Schluß einer Darstellung diese Lügen nach Möglichkeit aufzulösen" (IV, 241).

[35] "Die 'reinen' Religionen sind für eine kleine Schicht Hochstehender, während die Völker der Magien und Mythologien bedürfen" (Hermann Hesse, *Briefe* [erweiterte Ausgabe; Frankfurt am Main: Suhrkamp, 1964], p. 184).

[36] "Die Mythen der Bibel, wie alle Mythen der Menschheit, sind für

the substantive power is taken away, myth is of course no longer a cultural force; it is reduced to an aesthetic shape.

What we have observed up to this point can be simplified to the following generalization: Hesse's understanding of the word and concept "myth," up to roughly 1930, must be seen in the context of cultural history. He uses the term in conventional senses established by such authorities as Wagner, Nietzsche, and Jung and sanctioned by popular usage. But his attitude toward "myth" as a cultural power varies inversely with public opinion. During the period of public rationalism that dominated the Wilhelminian era, Hesse enjoyed his most irrational reverence for *Mythos*. But with the growing public irrationalism of the twenties—as attested by such works as Ludwig Klages's *Der Geist als Widersacher der Seele* (1929) [The Mind as Adversary of the Soul], Rudolf Kayser's *Die Zeit ohne Mythos* (1923) [An Age without Myth], or Arthur Liebert's *Mythus und Kultur* (1925)—he moved in the opposite direction until the term, in his vocabulary, is reduced to any "mythology" that is exploited to fool the people. His increasing sympathy for rationality is underscored in a letter of 1935 concerning his poem "Besinnung": "You guessed correctly that a transformation underlies the poem: namely, an incipient reflection on my heritage, which is Christian. But the impulse to formulate these reflections arose from the present controversy concerning 'biocentric' or 'logocentric' views of life, and I wanted to take a clear stand in favor of 'logocentric.'"[37] We see then that it would be a vast oversimplification to pin Hesse down as an antirationalist when, in fact, his attitude—as reflected in his use of

---

uns wertlos, solange wir sie nicht persönlich und für uns und unsere Zeit zu deuten wagen" (Ibid., p. 30).

[37] "Sie vermuten richtig, daß dem Gedicht eine Wandlung zu Grund liegt, nämlich eine beginnende 'Besinnung' auf meine Herkunft, welche christlich ist. Das Bedürfnis zur Formulierung aber entstand aus dem aktuellen Streit um 'biozentrische' oder 'logozentrische' Anschauungsart, und ich wollte mich deutlich zu 'logozentrisch' bekennen" (Ibid., p. 139).

the word "myth"—shifted radically in the course of the years.

Although the events of the twenties and thirties discredited myth for Hesse in a cultural sense, he did not drop the word from his vocabulary. But it is now used more carefully, in different and limited contexts: namely, in the neutral senses of literary criticism and philosophy. If myths no longer have absolute value, they still retain aesthetic structure: they become forms to be filled. This understanding opens the way for Hesse's aesthetic terminology. In an essay of 1928 he wrote: "A new poetic work begins to take form, for me, at the moment when a figure becomes visible to me which, for a while, can become the symbol and bearer of my experience, my thoughts, my problems. The appearance of this mythic person . . . is the creative instant from which everything arises."[38] Here the label "mythic" clearly implies the third sense of literary criticism—neither mythology nor archetype, but the product of the individual imagination. When, in this context, Hesse introduces the notion of reason, it is no longer in cultural opposition to myth, but as its complement: mythical imagination produces vivid images that expand rational conceptualization. It is for this reason, as he wrote to Karl Kerényi in 1944, that he now admires the great myths of mankind: "While, as a contemporary writer, one becomes so infinitely small in the face of this mythic world, one nevertheless feels confirmed and justified in the meaningfulness of one's activity, in poetic dreaming."[39] In another context he expressed a similar thought: "Poetry can exert itself as much as it wishes in order to put across one opinion or another; but it is

[38] "Eine neue Dichtung beginnt für mich in dem Augenblick zu entstehen, wo eine Figur mir sichtbar wird, welche für eine Weile Symbol und Träger meines Erlebens, meiner Gedanken, meiner Probleme werden kann. Die Erscheinung dieser mythischen Person . . . ist der schöpferische Augenblick, aus dem alles entsteht" (VII, 303).

[39] "Während man als Dichter von heute vor dieser mythischen Welt so unendlich klein wird, fühlt man sich doch im Sinn seines Tuns, im dichterischen Träumen, bestätigt und gerechtfertigt" (Hesse, *Briefe*, p. 210).

incapable of doing so; it lives and is effective only where it truly becomes poetry—that is, where it creates symbols."[40] Looking back at his own work, Hesse concludes that Demian and Frau Eva are mythic figures in this aesthetic sense: "They encompass and signify far more than is accessible to rational contemplation: they are magical conjurations."[41]

Although "myth" as a noun, as a magical power, is devalued in his thought, Hesse begins to regard it increasingly as a process that complements rational thought in all men. This is stated most clearly in an important essay entitled "Ein Stückchen Theologie" [A Bit of Theology], which Hesse wrote in 1932. In the first part of the essay Hesse outlines his belief in a triadic rhythm of humanization, which leads out of the innocence of childhood through the despair of consciousness to the transcendent and harmonious resolution of wisdom, where all opposites —including myth and reason—are reconciled. In the second half he turns to what he views as the two basic types of human being, which he categorizes as *die Vernünftigen* [the Rational] and *die Frommen* [the Pious]. Note how carefully he avoids the negative associations attached to such possible labels as the Mythic or the Irrational! Hesse warns us repeatedly—here in the essay as well as in his letters and novels—that any attempt to reduce mankind to such intellectual or rational systems must be taken with more than a grain of salt: "nothing can be more disastrous for the philosopher than a literal belief in any theory of types."[42] Yet Hesse finds his categories useful for preliminary

[40] "Die Dichtung aber kann sich anstrengen, soviel sie mag, um etwaige Meinungen durchzusetzen, sie vermag es nicht, sondern sie lebt und wirkt nur da, wo sie wirklich Dichtung ist, das heißt, wo sie Symbole schafft" (Ibid., p. 61).
[41] "Sie umschliessen und bedeuten weit mehr, als der rationalen Betrachtung zugänglich ist, sie sind magische Beschwörungen" (Ibid., p. 61).
[42] "Nichts kann dem Philosophen verhängnisvoller werden als der Buchstabenglaube an irgendeine Typenlehre" (VII, 394).

discrimination. The rationalist, he says, believes that he possesses the meaning of reality within his own mind, while the
pious man, in contrast, feels a reverence for a world order that
implies a superrational dimension. Whereas rational man is obsessed with systems, "the pious man easily becomes infatuated
with mythologies."[43] Beginning with this basic distinction between rational systems and "mythologies," Hesse dialectically
elaborates the differences between the two types, making it
absolutely clear that either extreme is self-defeating. "Rational
man rationalizes the world and does violence to it. He is always
inclined to be grimly serious."[44] "The pious man mythologizes
the world and, in the process, frequently fails to take it seriously
enough. He is always inclined to playfulness."[45] Finally, Hesse
confesses with considerable self-irony that he himself vacillates
between the two poles. At one moment, he says, he knows precisely to which type any historical figure belongs—and he
counts himself among the pious rather than among the rationalists. But in the next instant the entire system collapses. "Just a
moment ago I knew precisely that I was a pious man—and then
I detected, trait by trait, the characteristics of the rationalist—
and with especial clarity the most unpleasant characteristics."[46]
It is a mark of genius, he concludes, to feel a longing for the
opposite pole and to render full respect to the opposite type.
The supreme spiritual experience of which men are capable is
to effect a reconciliation between reason and reverence, "a
reciprocal acknowledgement of the great opposites."[47]

---

[43] "Der Fromme verliebt sich leicht in Mythologien" (VII, 398).

[44] "Der Vernünftige rationalisiert die Welt und tut ihr Gewalt an. Er
neigt stets zu grimmigen Ernst" (VII, 397).

[45] "Der Fromme mythologisiert die Welt und nimmt sie häufig darüber
nicht ernst genug. Er neigt stets etwas zum Spielen" (VII, 399).

[46] "Eben noch wußte ich genau, daß ich ein Frommer sei—und nun
entdeckte ich Zug um Zug an mir die Merkmale des Vernunftmenschen
und besonders deutlich die unangenehmsten Merkmale" (VII, 395).

[47] "Ein Sich-als-Gleich-Erkennen der grossen Gegensätze" (VII, 400).

To comprehend the meaning of Myth and Reason in Hesse's life and thought, then, we must differentiate clearly among three basic frames of reference. Up until roughly 1930, he reacted to the word *Myth* in the senses given by contemporary cultural history—in *Peter Camenzind* with a positive response and after *Demian* in an increasingly negative reaction against cultural developments. After he rejected the word in its cultural sense, however, Hesse continued to use it—more cautiously and almost invariably supplying his own definition—in two other contexts. He employed it aesthetically to suggest the nonreferential implications and connotations that can emerge from the images of art. And he rejected the assumption of contemporary cultural philosophy that myth and reason are antagonistic forces: he understood them, rather, as complementary processes of understanding that are inherent in all mankind. It is the meaning of *Der Steppenwolf*, surely, that Harry Haller learn to accept both, indeed, all aspects of his personality: bourgeois and wolf, reason and myth. By the same token, *Narziss und Goldmund* amounts to a symbolic projection of Hesse's belief in the complementarity of the two basic types: the rationalizing priest Narziss and the mythifying artist Goldmund. It would be a fruitful exercise, in fact, to consider all of Hesse's later novels in the light of the categories Myth and Reason as he defined them in his essay "Ein Stückchen Theologie." One of the deficiencies of the Castalian existence, against which Joseph Knecht rebels in *Das Glasperlenspiel*, is surely its suppression of the mythic imagination for the sake of an increasingly sterile rationality.

These prolegomena have by no means exhausted the topic Hesse: Myth and Reason, nor did they set out to do so. It was my intention solely to suggest some of the terminological and methodological difficulties that complicate this problem and to adumbrate certain possibly worthwhile directions of future inquiry. We have seen that outside the strict contexts of eth-

nology and literary criticism the vocables Myth and Reason
assume pronounced values that vary depending upon the standpoint of the speaker. Now it is a great mistake, I believe, to
underestimate the impact that habits of language can exert upon
our thought. It is mere self-delusion to believe that our objectivity is so serene that we can fully escape the magnetic attraction of powerful conventions of thought. Specifically, in our
society the opposition of Myth to Reason is so pervasive that it
affects our thinking more often than we care to admit. To use
the fashionable analogy from physics—Heisenberg's indeter-
minacy principle—the observer intrudes unwittingly into the
field of observation through the very act of observation. At the
moment when I undertake to analyze Hesse within the frame-
work of Myth and Reason, my results can all too easily be influenced by my own point of view. If I consider myself highly
rational in my outlook, then I will not have much appreciation
for a writer in whose thought and works I detect qualities that
I identify as "mythic"—and vice versa. We can neutralize the
effect of these habits of language and thought to a certain extent if we proceed with a conscious awareness of our own point
of view and its limitations. But to illustrate how we can be mis-
led if we fail to take these factors into account, let us consider
two recent articles on Hesse. I have purposely chosen, instead
of detached analyses, popular pieces committed, respectively,
to attacking and defending Hesse.

In a recent article in *Look* magazine (February 23, 1971),
Senior Editor Frank Trippett sought to explain the reasons underlying what he calls the current "Hesse Trip" among the
young in this country. Trippett does not attempt to conceal his
disenchantment with what parades under the label of rationality
today. "Rationality passes over the threshold to lunacy. . . . In
the shadow of the works of rationality, it is reasonable for men
to seek joy beyond reason." It follows almost logically, therefore, that Trippett is attracted primarily by the "mythic" aspect

of Hesse's works, which he sees veiled in the garb of Jungian archetypes. "A primer on Jung would be the best preface to any Hesse tale," Trippett observes. "In each, the hero follows the Jungian way, struggling from dissatisfaction with the *persona*, increasing awareness of submerged *shadow* beings within, into the quest, the grapplings, the confusions, the symbols of the animus-anima swarming to the fore, swarming among those other Jungian things, the archetypal beings that dwell in what Jung called the *collective unconscious*." Given his intoxication with myth and his hostility toward rationality, it is hardly surprising that Trippett refers with explicit distaste to an article that had appeared a few months earlier in the *Yale Review* (Spring, 1970)—Jeffrey Sammons's "Notes on the Germanization of American Youth."

Sammons proclaims an attitude of "pragmatism and ideologically skeptical realism," but for all practical purposes it is identical with a kind of no-nonsense rationalism. Accordingly, Sammons can barely suppress his contempt when he speaks of the "anti-modern and Romantic-mystical elements in Hesse's works." And among the most unforgivable attributes of Hesse's soft-minded irrationalism is the myth of the lost paradise, which Sammons calls "a kind of national neurosis that is related in some as yet undefined way to the perpetually disappointing conditions of German society." Sammons's rationalistic hostility toward myth is further signaled by his unwitting debasement of the word itself when he speaks, for instance, of Hesse's "hypostasis of the myth of the golden-hearted whore in *Steppenwolf.*"

The point is not whether one agrees with Sammons or with Trippett; indeed, it is impossible to agree fully with either writer without accepting an intellectual position of extreme rationalism or extreme antirationalism. We observe simply that myth and reason have here become rhetorical whips with which they scourge Hesse, society, and one another, rather than analytical tools with which they come to grips with a common object.

In the first place, both Trippett and Sammons force Hesse into
an attitude of irrationalism: for the one this is reason for ap-
proval and for the other it is cause for contempt. Yet we have
seen that Hesse would be loath to accept this position under
either condition. The critic's own commitment, in other words,
has biased his view of the object. But there is, secondly, an additional paradox: for their attitude also affects the critics' assessment of their own society. Sammons finds Hesse's attitude
"unthinkable in Anglo-Saxon culture, but not uncommon in Germany"; and he sets himself up—if we permit ourselves to expand
his own metaphor—as an intellectual plumber who must
end "the superficial seepage of the German tradition into the
adolescent and student subculture." (Paradoxically, the kindred
spirits of reason that Sammons invokes in his crusade against the
Germanization of American youth are Lessing and Heine.)
Sammons, then, attacks Hesse because his irrationalism and
mythic attitudes have "a decidedly German aspect as compared
with the pragmatism, liberalism, tolerance, and democracy that
we like to think belong to our own heritage." Curiously enough,
Trippett's enthusiasm for Hesse is strengthened precisely because he feels that Hesse's "mythic" qualities are so closely akin
to the American temperament. Trippett grew up in the American South, which—he says—is just as "remote and mystical and
obscure and impenetrable" as anything in Hesse. Rather than
seeing in Hesse's works, as Sammons does, a hostile and alien
quality, Trippett argues that "perhaps the East is not as far
from the West as some of our public monitors assume." Sammons's self-proclaimed rationalism causes him to see Hesse's use
of myth as reprehensible and un-American—an insidious fifth
column of the Spirit against which he has mounted his own
campaign for cultural embargo. Trippett's distrust of reason
brings him to the very opposite conclusions: in his eyes Hesse's
mythic quality constitutes his principal appeal and makes his
works just as American as apple pie or—given the regional bias

perhaps we should say—Southern fried chicken. Sammons and Trippett, in short, do not ask us judiciously to weigh the pros and cons in order to arrive at an objective opinion; rather, they harass us into taking a loyalty oath for or against Myth—we must declare ourselves against Hesse as a foreign subversive agent, or for him as a founding father of the American way of life.

If no writer but Hesse were involved the problem would not be so serious. But in fact the attitude toward Myth and Reason that we have traced in Hesse's development is so characteristic of many writers of his generation that it might be called paradigmatic—or even "mythic"—in its significance. The works of Thomas Mann, Hugo von Hofmannsthal, and Hermann Broch, for instance, show precisely the same pattern: an early willingness to accept the notion of myth with all its problematic associations is succeeded by a disenchantment with myth as a cultural force and a more sophisticated terminological differentiation. Karl Kerényi recollects that in Germany *entre deux guerres* the word *Mythos* grew to become "an incomprehensible power— at once ridiculous and ominous, yet acknowledged even by someone like Thomas Mann."[48] In his correspondence with Kerényi, in turn, Mann concedes that, like so many of his contemporaries, he had participated in a joyous "return of the European spirit to the highest, the mythic realities."[49] But he goes on to point out that the "irrational fashion" of the twenties, from which this unreasoning mythophilia stemmed, all too frequently involved a disregard, indeed a discarding, of those very qual-

[48] "Einer unbegreiflichen, zugleich lächerlichen und verhängnisvollen, doch auch von Thomas Mann anerkannten Macht" (From Kerényi's introduction to Thomas Mann—Karl Kerényi, *Gespräch in Briefen* (Zurich: Rhein-Verlag, 1960), p. 20.

[49] "Rückkehr des europäischen Geistes zu den höchsten, den mythischen Realitäten." Mann's letters to Kerényi are cited according to the text in Mann's *Gesammelte Werke in zwölf Bänden* (S. Fischer, 1960); here, XI, 631.

ities that make men into human beings. Mann's initial fascination with the power of myth, with all its Nietzschean and Jungian associations, gives way to skepticism as he sees the ravages
perpetrated in the name of irrationality and myth. The position
that he ultimately reaches during the thirties is practically identical with the "logocentric" attitude that Hesse proclaimed when
the world around him became increasingly "biocentric," irrational, and mythological. "I am a man of equilibrium," Mann
wrote. "I instinctively lean to the left when the boat threatens to
capsize to the right—and vice-versa."[50] As a result, he regarded it
as one of his main duties, in the thirties, to rationalize myth by
means of psychological demythification. As he wrote to Kerényi:
"Psychology is the means of wresting myth out of the hands of
these fascist obscurantists and of 're-functioning' it into something human."[51]

It would behoove us as critics and scholars to aspire to the
same degree of differentiation as the writers with whom we
deal. But we can do this only if we resist the lure of language
that seduces us into ideological positions. In the last analysis,
both mythophilia and mythophobia are irrational attitudes to
the extent that any excessive love or fear is irrational. If we can
learn anything from ethnology, it is perhaps the lesson that
myth and reason are modes of perception and expression that
coexist inherently in all men, rather than antagonistic forces that
claim our loyalty. Myth without the controlling force of reason
can rapidly swell into a mindless and formless euphoria, while

[50] "Ich bin ein Mensch des Gleichgewichts. Ich lehne mich instinktiv
nach links, wenn der Kahn rechts zu kentern droht,—und umgekehrt"
(Ibid., XI, 632).

[51] "Denn tatsächlich ist Psychologie das Mittel, den Mythos den faschi-
stistischen Dunkelmännern aus den Händen zu nehmen und ihn ins
Humane 'umzufunktionieren' " (Ibid., XI, 651). Regarding Mann's ambivalent attitude toward myth, see Henry Hatfield, "Myth versus Secular-
ism: Religion in Thomas Mann's *Joseph*," in Hatfield's *Crisis and Continuity in Modern German Fiction: Ten Essays* (Ithaca, N.Y.: Cornell University Press, 1969), pp. 78–89.

reason without myth degenerates into sterile formalism—in literature as well as in life. The finest poetry of all ages, surely, has been produced at that delicate point of equilibrium where the power of imagination is channeled into its most effective form by the force of rationality—where myth is enhanced by reason. This, as we have seen, was Hesse's view. And it was also the case, I believe, with Hesse's own work at its best.

MYTH *AND* REASON?

A *Round-Table Discussion*

with

Hough-Lewis Dunn, Ph.D. candidate,
Department of Germanic Languages,
The University of Texas at Austin

Jost Hermand, Vilas Research Professor
Department of German,
The University of Wisconsin at Madison

Wilson M. Hudson, Professor
Department of English, The University of Texas at Austin

Lee B. Jennings, Professor
Department of German,
University of Illinois at Chicago Circle

Edgar C. Polomé, Professor
Germanic Languages, Linguistics, Oriental and African Languages,
The University of Texas at Austin

Henry A. Selby, Associate Professor
Department of Anthropology, The University of Texas at Austin

A. Leslie Willson, Professor
Department of Germanic Languages,
The University of Texas at Austin

Theodore Ziolkowski, Professor
Department of Germanic Languages and Literatures,
Princeton University

J. Christopher Middleton, Professor
Department of Germanic Languages,
The University of Texas at Austin
Moderator

MIDDLETON: We are in an aleatory situation, because I don't think any of us know specifically what we are going to discuss, although much might be said about many of the things that have been said so far, both to extend and to clarify the issues involved in this binary opposition, Myth and Reason. We only reached, with Mr. Ziolkowski's lecture, something like a definite understanding of the differences involved in the usage, particularly of the word "myth," but in no less an important way, of the word "reason." Maybe I should recapitulate by reading you the summary, which Mr. Ziolkowski gave in his lecture:

> Literary criticism uses the term "myth" in at least three ways which are unacceptable to the more rigorous understanding of ethnology. All objections of terminology aside, however, these three approaches have produced valuable insights in the study of literary works generally and of Hesse's novels in particular. But if we now consider the specific topic of this Symposium, it turns out that even these definitions current in literary criticism are not strictly germane. For we have been asked to deal with the subject of Myth *and* Reason in German literature. But a curious thing happens to the word "myth" when it is juxtaposed with the notion of "reason": It takes on still another meaning that is only tenuously related to the primary definition of ethnology and the secondary senses of criticism.

Now, from that paragraph, I think that one should mark out certain areas, each of which has its own criteria, its own structure. There is an area in that particular paper called "primary myth." This is presumably a highly complex area, where ethnologists reign supreme, but, unless I am mistaken, would be inclined almost to desist nowadays from speaking of "myth" as such, but would be inclined to differentiate much more finely and to think in terms of specific myths of specific societies, at least to get around the monistic delusion that there is such a thing as "the myth" or even "a myth." There is a second area, that in which we stand as heirs to Western civilization, namely, the area in which most of the myths known to us are, in

effect, already literary versions of myths which had their origins in
a preliterate or oral tradition. It is an odd feature that the Greek and
even the Egyptian myths which we inherit in the West are already
written down and—in some cases—are highly elaborate literary versions of tales which must have been told for centuries if not millennia
before this writing-down occurred. In other words, although we
think of the Olympian gods as "mythic" gods, and some of us may
even think of the *Odyssey* as a great protomyth of Western civilization, these are already poems, and it's extremely difficult to find anything like the ritual basis on which the *Odyssey* might be founded, if
you think the *Odyssey* is a myth and you think that myth is rooted
or related in some way to a rite or ritual. There is also a third area,
the area which I would be inclined, after Mr. Hermand's talk, to give
a new name to and call it "unmyth." This is the domain of pseudodoxy, *pseudodoxia epidemica* as they used to be called in the seventeenth century, epidemic false beliefs. These are, of course, myths;
but I think it is unfortunate that the word "myth" has become attached to the self-delusion, the fakery, and the propaganda, the
manipulation area of mythology, which is one of the major diseases of
our time and to which we are, alas, more exposed than we are to the
original information which is enshrined in primary myth or even in
the great literary versions of ancient myths.

Now may I introduce Mr. Henry Selby at this point. Henry Selby
is an ethnologist who has worked collecting myths among the Zapo-
tec Indians in Mexico. He is also widely read in the structuralist
studies of myths, mythologems generally; he says "Lévi-Strauss is
my hero" (maybe that is a myth, too). I'd be very interested to hear
from him, ever so briefly, or so long as he likes, an account of how a
literary study of literary myth seems to him, as a person whose major
interest is the primary myth, or the myth of the ethnologist.

SELBY: I think that the major difference between the literary point
of view and the anthropologist's point of view (on myth) concerns
what we regard as myth. While I listened to the speakers I found
myself in a discomfiting disagreement with them, wanting all the
time to say, "that's not myth at all," and remembering Sapir's distinctions between "genuine" and "spurious" cultural forms. It is quite
clear to an ethnologist that myths encode deep truths about human
experience, and that they are accepted that way by their tellers and
listeners. I don't think the same could be said for Madison Avenue
productions. To an ethnologist, who tries to savor the experience and

the ideology of the people he studies, myths are timeless productions concerned with ultimate questions, and I don't think that when all of us talk about myth we mean the same thing in this regard. While I was listening, I was trying to think of examples of modern myths that I would regard as proper subjects for study and analysis, and I think that science is one such example. Listeners and tellers pay rapt attention to science. They take it seriously and believe it applies to them in their lives, is timeless, and encodes profound truths about the human condition. Those of you who, like me, were abroad at the time of the U.S. moon landing will recall our sophisticated amusement at the ingenuousness of the gullibility of peoples of other countries when it was reported (in Rio, for example) that no one believed that a moon landing was taking place, because the television reception was much too good, or the report (from Lima) that it couldn't have been much of a trick because everybody knew that the moon was so close (and curiously similar to the terrain around the Peruvian capital). We smiled, because we believed in the moon landing. It was a reality to us, and we shared in Walter Cronkite's tearful awe at the mystery of the knowledge and technology that made it possible. Walter Cronkite was creating modern myth before our eyes.

But there's more to my point than this. For an ethnologist, myth-making and sciencing are not dissimilar activities. And to an ethnologist the suggestion that there is some kind of useful distinction to be made between myth and reason is unacceptable. Science is an elaborate ideology based in unprovable axioms about the world—and so is myth. Science involves the classification of discrete categories of events and invents categorical distinctions for its own purposes; so does myth. Science involves the elaboration of very formal systems, the invention of languages that relate classes of events, and so does myth. The distinction between myth and science lies in the way these things are done. Science is more highly constrained than myth. A scientist rests his case on the assertion that there exists a high probability that relationships which he obtains ideologically will have empirical correspondences in the real world. A myth makes no such claims; in fact myths constantly play with relationships (like the "mad scientist") and speculate about things that were, but are no more, things that cannot be, and things that never were, but are. There *is* reason in myth, just as there is reason in science. It is not the same reasoning, but nevertheless it is reason. Myths, as Lévi-Strauss has pointed out, build up intellectual structures from the concrete things-at-hand around the teller of myth, and use a logic of the concrete, whereas the fundamental intellectual act of the scientist is the distinction between the known (empirically) and the postulated-but-not-known of the theorist.

So, for me at least, many of the connotations of the word "myth" are quite different from those for the other contributors to the symposium.

MIDDLETON: Looking at the thing from a literary point of view, myth is a sacred story about origins, not a provable story about causes. There is very little merit in it as a scientific theory. On the other hand, is it science that manages our lives for us without our knowing it? I doubt that, to start with; I also doubt the likelihood of science being able to provide more than an inhabitable context. I think myth, for a person who lives within the terms of reference of a primary myth or a sacred story, is a totally different process. It is not necessarily magical, but it is something you can play with. Life is play, or it is craft, things like that, if there *are* other things like that. Whereas the scientific context immediately fixes you; you're deprived, in a sense, not just of freedom from day to day, but of the deeper freedom of play in the sources of your being. I think there are differences here.

SELBY: No, I'm not saying that there is *no* difference between science on the one hand and myth on the other. But I would say there is a good deal of similarity between mythopoesis and scientific theorizing. Myth is a medium of thought, or of discourse, just as science is. The logical forms are different, but both attempt to make statements about the nature of the world, about causation, about concordance, and they do it in not dissimilar ways, if we think on the general level.

MIDDLETON: Well, according to Ernst Cassirer, there *is* a difference, but Myth and Reason are not incompatible. Reasoning and mythmaking share certain features, but there are also differences in direction. I think, theoretically speaking, in fact, it's very nice and cozy to think that mythic ideation (which is related to language forming and language utterance) and reasoning, are sister processes. In practice, of course, this does not prove to be the case in the third realm of "unmyth" or pseudodoxies, where there is a tremendous challenge for people who believe that rational modes of life are more humane than irrational ones and who do the critical work of eroding the false myths which surround us and penetrate the very ground on which we stand as human beings. I would like to know what you have to say to that, Mr. Hermand.

HERMAND: I would actually reject what Mr. Selby proposed here. I don't want to continue as the *enfant terrible*, but I think this is a formalistic or structural approach without making any kind of a distinction. I would rather stick to the concept which Mr. Middleton outlined in the beginning: the three stages of mythmaking—primary myth, literary manifestations as the second phase, and then what he called the "unmyth." I would put them in a chronological order, not really strictly in terms of Hegel or some Hegelian idea, but in some kind of a neo-Hegelian concept. I think there is some truth to the notion that a mythical interpretation precedes the religious interpretation, that the religious interpretation of the world is already a sort of rational structuring of mythical elements, the first attempt to bring this mythical interpretation into rational order, as in Thomas Aquinas, for instance. The next phase would be the rational interpretation. I would see a necessary historical development in this process, from a mythical interpretation of the world which is still unable to give a rational explanation—of why it rains, for instance —(or just gives some kind of magical force behind everything), to the religious view of the world as a mixture of rationalism and magic, and then, finally, to the rational interpretation since the sixteenth century, or in Greek antiquity, much earlier. I would see this as a historical development and not just observe certain formalistic similarities between concepts which both include reasoning.

ZIOLKOWSKI: I'd like to say a word for ethnology . . .

HERMAND: Okay, ethnology has its place in this because ethnology is concerned with primary myths; it has a historical interest in primary myths as the Darwinists had a historical interest in the development of the species.

ZIOLKOWSKI: But I think that no matter where we look we find myth and rationality existing side by side. You, Mr. Selby, didn't like the word "primitive," but the primitive tribe that scientifically plants its crops at the same time is capable of mythically rationalizing what it's doing, or of interpreting what it's doing in a mythic way. In the twentieth century we are similarly capable of great feats of what we call rationality, and, at the same time, we are also capable of total beliefs in myths. And here I am tempted to believe that science is

one of our greatest myths and that science fiction is the equivalent of
our mythmaking today. Similarly, when you look at the Greeks: un-
questionably in the fifth century there were still some conservative
Greeks who took the gods seriously, just as today there are still some
people with fundamental religious beliefs. There were others, such
as Aeschylus and Sophocles, who used them in a more detached,
ironic way for mythmaking, mythopoesis, that is, for the purpose of
art. At the same time, there were people, like Socrates, who rationally rejected all of them and said it's not really worth spending one's
time on. In other words, I think, whether you look at "primitive"
society, early society, or contemporary society, you can find myth
and reason coexisting simultaneously, and in some kind of fruitful
balance. Things get bad when people start believing their myths too
much or start trusting too greatly in their technology and their science. But I can't agree that there's a historical progression and that
we are moving up along the road toward perfection, leaving myths
behind and moving toward a greater rationality. Nothing I see in
history or in contemporary America suggests that to me.

JENNINGS: I am puzzled as to how you distinguish between true
and false myths, since myths do not have literal truth, but always
have some psychic truth. How can one be true and the other false?

MIDDLETON: Well, one probably has to work from case to case,
using a very vigilant, critical posture, which isn't a posture here, but
an act of interrogation for whatever one comes across. I think there
is one distinction: the likelihood that anything that can reasonably
be called myth does have a structure; whereas that which is "unmyth" or pseudodoxy tends to collapse everything into simplifica-
tions. It would require a vigilant, critical sense, which is wary of
anything that has the whiff of falseness about it; a kind of sensibility
which is not just aesthetic or sophisticated, but which does have a
sense of what is a structure and what isn't, an informed sensibility
(informed in the original sense of the word). Also a mind which is
avid for not being distorted by information which is pumped out
into the air by media—a mind which is avid for the original information, which is what the *Urkunde* is; which is what a myth
is. I think it's a virtual schooling of oneself, training one's nose
to actually suggest whether there are any things beyond the
structure and the collapsing. I couldn't go any further than that.

HUDSON: May I mention Lévy-Bruhl here? He spent his life investigating the thesis that the mind of primitive man is prelogical: it does not operate as the mind of civilized man. Myth is the product of this kind of mind. But, then again, he later recanted and said: The mind of primitive man operates in precisely the same way as the mind of civilized man. Now the British anthropologists liked the etiological interpretation. They saw an attempt on the part of primitive man to explain the causes of this, that, and the other. They are guilty of anachronisms, reading the spiritual history of mankind backward. That's what they would have been interested in, the causes of things, if they had been placed back several thousand years before.

But there's a great deal more to myth than the desire to explain why this, that, or the other is so, more than a "just-so story." I would like to go on just a little bit further in this matter of reason and myth. I'd like to mention a book by Rudolf Otto called *The Idea of the Holy*.[1] Otto's inquiry was into just what is holy; he was interested in myth only in a secondary way. The components of holiness are a feeling that the holy manifestation is more-than-life, the "great other," and that the person who is experiencing the feeling of holiness is in the presence of a tremendous mystery. Otto coined a word— "numinous"—which has had great usage since his time, to express these components of the feeling of "altogether other," "greater than I," and "the tremendous mystery." Otto begins by saying that the more you are able to define a concept in words, the more rationalistic you make the concept; and the very essence of the holy is that it cannot be reduced to conceptual language. Then he goes on to distinguish the components. Both C. G. Jung and Mircea Eliade have made great use of Otto and his language, including the word "numinous." Eliade conceived of the mythological as an appearance—manifestation—of a power or of a god or of holiness (in such terms as kratophany, hierophany, theophany). This is the essence of a mythological situation. Of course, Jung uses "numinous" as a means of detecting the presence of the mythological, by using the responses or reactions of those who are experiencing the holy or the mythological. It is inevitable that in such a Symposium as ours we would use the word "myth" in different senses and that there would be longings expressed

[1] Rudolf Otto, *The Idea of the Holy: An Inquiry into the Non-rational Factor in the Idea of the Divine and its Relation to the Rational*, trans. John W. Harvey, 2d ed. (London, New York: Oxford University Press, 1957).

by ourselves or others that we have one sense for myth or a handful of senses, and that we could confine ourselves to those senses. I notice on the table a book by Henry A. Murray.[2] He made a most heroic attempt to define myth in the most rationalistic and systematic form. He had numbered paragraphs and alternates, combinations of this and combinations of that; but what it comes down to, and I am simplifying a great deal, is that there be present at least one supernatural being and one supernatural event. That doesn't leave much for myth, but still you will find him in agreement, that the essence of a myth is the holy, or the experience of a "greater-than-I."

MIDDLETON: I recall a political caricature by George Grosz, from about 1922. It was a picture of a huge Wotan with helmet aloft. The Teutonic giant was there, who looked extremely holy, and in front of him all kinds of *petit bourgois* doing pious things—kneeling, praying, bowing, and the rest; and, behind the god, there was a man in a top hat, the insignia of the capitalist, turning the handle. This is where the trouble begins, when the pseudo-numinous is held up to be the "absolutely other," or the "big brother," as is sometimes the case. And the human emotions which need religious devotion are bent, turned around, so that they come blindly and uncritically to look upon this "absolutely other," or this numinous object, as that which can save them. By structure I meant a system of relationships, and I think that the Wotan figure and the capitalist behind him turning the handle (or whatever kind of "big brother" may be behind the scenes) do not constitute a true relationship or a complex relationship of any kind. This is precisely the area in which the problems occur. How can one tell the true numen from the pseudo numen?

JENNINGS: I wonder if one of the ways might be the survival power of the myth: if it's really numinous, then it will eventually prevail. But if it's just somebody turning the crank . . .

WILLSON: May I make a comment? I remember, in one lecture, the statement was made that the beginning of myth was connected with ritual. I wonder if that isn't a kind of manipulation? The priests have turned the crank there; maybe it was someone like Homer, someone who was a poet. Maybe it wasn't just a poet, but maybe it was the poet-priest. But is there in primitive societies a manipulation of the ritual through myth, or vice versa?

[2] Henry A. Murray, ed., *Myth and Mythmaking* (1960; paperback ed., Boston: Beacon Press, 1968).

SELBY: I can't speak for "primitive" traditional society, for of that I am quite ignorant, but there is this old argument, of course, about the relationship between myth and ritual. I routinely take the position that they are really quite distinct. I have a myth that I spin to myself about the creation of myth, and it has to do with such elemental things as the passage from nature to culture, the separation of man, the animal, from the other animals; it has to do with the invention of such arbitrary forms of classification as the classification of people: people whom I can marry, people with whom I can have sexual relations, incest taboos. So many myths that I'm familiar with —and this may be a product of my own ignorance—have to do with origins of some kind. They try to speculate about something being there that wasn't there before, but they're not scientific in the sense that they say there is a causal chain here. The epistemology of myths is extremely complicated; it switches levels all the time. You notice this particularly when you're talking to people about their myths, and you say, Is that true? and they reply as if to say, No, that's not true in the sense you mean it; but it's a kind of axiomatic substatement on that level and you can't reduce it to another level. Don't you know any philosophy of science? It seems to me that myths are intellectual productions, and they do impart and code basic paradoxes, but they don't encode them in a straightforward fashion. They pose riddles for which there are no answers; and they pose answers for which there are no riddles. They pose things that were, things that could have been, things that might be, and things that can never be. They play with these all the time, and they deal with and transform basic structures of reality, which are deeply embedded in the human consciousness, much as the syntactical forms, the base rules of our linguistic utterances, are embedded very deeply. I would tend to distinguish between myth and ritual, in the sense that I think ritual is a partial realization in a different form, in a collective form, quite often, in a form that is constrained by bodily movements, by verse form and things like that, whereas myth is much more free-ranging.

WILLSON: My question really was: If myth is used in ritual, is it manipulated?

SELBY: Yes.

HUDSON: I would like to state Susanne K. Langer's solution to this problem.[3] Myth is a verbal expression, and ritual is a motor expression; and they both express the same thing. So you do not have to worry about which comes first, or about any problem of manipulation. The idea that myth or religion could have been created by cynical priests is just preposterous. Dryden had that idea a long time ago, but religion couldn't have been invented in order to hornswoggle the savages.

POLOMÉ: With relation to the function of myths, I would also tend to agree with Mr. Selby in saying that they try to explain origins, and that's where you find them, mostly. This may tie in with some of the things that Mr. Hermand pointed out. As a matter of fact, if we look at Indo-European myth, we find that it is connected with the origin of the world and the organization of the Indo-European society. We find that, whereas in certain groups, it remains a myth, as such, in other groups euhemerism changes it totally and it becomes pure history. And, within a certain group, we find that something that appears as a myth at a certain period and is very nicely structured, with a series of contrasts—deep contrasts in the spiritual life, in attitudes of man versus nature, and so on—is reconstructed in real romance at a later period. We have a beautiful example in the Germanic world with the Saga of Hadingus, which starts as a pure myth and ends up as practically a novella in Saxo Grammaticus. This is a frequent phenomenon.

When Mr. Hermand, in his lecture, was talking about the fringe-area people who were revitalizing the Germanic mythology and using it, we have also to keep in mind that some very serious people did this a long time before Nazism. It's obvious that, for instance, German archaeology played a decisive role in this. I have here in front of me a book that was published for, I think, the eighth time, in 1941, which quotes a passage of Adolf Hitler, in 1934, paraphrasing the statements of Gustav Kossinna in a book written in 1912, in which this famous archaeologist states that the Germanic past would justify all kinds of political attitudes at the beginning of World War I.[4] The theme was taken up by Hitler in 1934 to say that Germans didn't owe anything to the Greeks and the Romans, for they had a

---

[3] Susanne K. Langer, *Philosophy in a New Key: A Study in the Symbolism of Reason, Rite, and Art*, 3d ed. (Cambridge, Mass.: Harvard University Press, 1957).

[4] Gustav Kossinna, *Die deutsche Vorgeschichte: eine hervorragend nationale Wissenschaft* (1912; Johann Ambrosius Barth, Leipzig, 1941).

culture which was well-established a thousand years before Rome was established. This idea was taken over by very serious people, and it was difficult not to assume the truth of their statements, because they were presented by scholars who had authority. It was not only a German phenomenon, but the idea of the glorification of the Germanic past also started in Scandinavia. The responsibility of such people as Vilhelm Grønbech, for instance, in the idealization of the Germanic hero and the *bon sauvage germanique* is indeed very great, too. So I think this European background should also be taken into consideration when we discuss twentieth-century myth.

HUDSON: I think Mr. Hermand was entirely justified in speaking of an ideological activity as mythological. The reigning myth was the idea of the "chosen people," that is, there was some kind of destiny, something greater than any one person or greater than the people, according to these crackpots (as they were properly called), who had chosen the German race for great things, for a great destiny. The pattern is mythological, because we have a numinous element, albeit a mistaken one. There was some aspect of deception of others, but it was not just a propagandistic matter arranged beforehand by certain debased people who decided that they would work something out in order to delude the people. This was called for; there are historical reasons for it and there are psychic reasons for it, likewise. One of the best interpretations of popular psychomanifestations is an article by C. G. Jung on Wotan worship,[5] and he was greatly influenced by the fact that there was a recurrence of Wotan worship in Germany. It caused him great consternation when he saw the first signs of it coming along. And these people were not in a conspiracy, like propagandists: they were deluding themselves as much as they were deluding the German people.

MIDDLETON: I think Socrates hit the nail on the head when he said that there is no point in bothering about all the extraneous stuff if I do not first know myself. This was his reason for refusing to do what we're doing here. That's about the best reason that could be given for declining, in spite of its intrinsic interest, the nonsense of the *Stoff* [content], because one never lives long enough really even to know oneself. But this also is the sore point, because after all,

---

[5] C. G. Jung, "Wotan," in *Collected Works of C. G. Jung* (New York: Pantheon Books, 1964, 10, 179–193) [Vol. 10 is entitled: *Civilization in Transition*].

self-knowledge, now, does involve the inspection of one's own archetypes; getting to know them, becoming their familiar, rather than
having them as one's familiars, so that you haunt them and you can
control them by haunting them rather than them haunting you. It's
being haunted that introduces the element of belief as a form of
delusion, self-delusion.

DUNN: You referred to Socrates and this brings to mind Plato's
Republic, in which Socrates debunks the great tragedies of the
Grecian world; and if these are false myths, according to Socrates,
what does this do to our great literature? In the *Republic* there's
really no place for literature. It seems as if Socrates had a bias
against it. And he had thought about it to some extent, contrary to
what he says in Plato's dialogue *Phaedrus*.

MIDDLETON: Well, Mr. Selby happens also to be a classical scholar,
so I'll let him speak to that.

SELBY: Well, I wouldn't want to speak to that. I wonder if there's
any point—I really don't know—in distinguishing between myth,
which I keep insisting is an intellectual production, and something
which Bronislaw Malinowski would call "charter," which we might
reinterpret as social ideology. Charter, being a very constrained form,
a very ephemeral aspect of mythmaking (it is very liable to change,
not only in its surface structure, the way all myths change, but in its
deep structure as well), is very much tied to a particular sociological
order. And, as I was saying before, myths fancify about things that
might have been, and also about things that cannot be, while in fact
these kinds of charters, or social ideologies, classify what can be
and what ought to be. The pseudodoxies we were talking about are
more or less implicit charters that lay out in a more detailed sense
the everyday sorts of laws and the everyday sorts of structures that
we ought to live in and are living in, and they justify, in that sense,
the social order. I find it useful to make that distinction.

ZIOLKOWSKI: There's another distinction that I find it useful to
make, and people are probably tired of hearing me say so, but I'll
say it again—namely, the distinction between the thing and the
name. Nobody in this room would deny that there is some such thing
that may be known as myth. And I, personally, think that I, as a
critic and scholar of literature, stand to learn most from anthropology, ethnology, and history of religion about the thing itself, the
phenomenon of myth. A great deal of discussion has gone on; I've

learned some things here at this table in the past hour that are of great interest to me and that deal with the thing—the concept of myth. But, at the same time, undeniably, there's also a word, one word in German, one in English; and the word is not always necessarily related to the thing. Furthermore, I believe that the word has a history of its own that can be traced objectively and defined, and it comes out having no particular connection with myth in the primary sense of the ethnologist. It's no accident, I think, that in the Nazi period the word "myth" rather than "idea" or "thought" was used to characterize the ideology of the Fascists. It's a word to conjure with; like "progress," "liberty," "democracy." The word has different meanings for different societies, and it has received in the German language certain meanings that have not necessarily anything whatsoever to do with the primary myth of ethnology. Perhaps it confuses the issue to try to ask the question whether, or to what extent, twentieth-century myth is like the ethnologist's myth. The question should rather be: What magic did the word "myth" assume and how did it assume this magic so that it was an attractive vocable for men who wanted, by rhetorical means, to whip up the emotional or irrational frenzy of the people to whom they were appealing? And then the parallel question would be: By what process, historical-semantic process, did it happen in the United States that the opposite took place—that we use the word "myth" here for different rhetorical purposes? I think the two words, *Mythos* in German and *myth* in English, have a history that literary critics, scholars, linguists can trace, and it's an interesting history in itself. I'm not at all convinced, however, that it's the same as myth, the thing. I think that we are dealing with concepts that define themselves almost internally and autonomously.

HERMAND: Yes, this is a point well taken. I think, in the context of Myth and Reason, our primary interest should be in just the third groups you mentioned, the so-called unmyths, because these are the things which we are really surrounded with. We are not dealing with the original, primary myth any more in our society. We are surrounded with this debased kind of "unmyth." And these are the things we have to fight against, because these are the things that are always being manipulated and forced upon us. We see how they are manipulated, what kind of reactionary forces are always behind these manipulations with "unmyth," which are not only restricted to the concept of fascism. I think that was a very good example Mr.

Ziolkowski gave this morning from the article in *Look* on Hermann Hesse.[6] What kind of myth-manipulation was taking place here? This man seemed to be praising debased irrationality as the new fad. There I see the real myth-manipulation: trying to disorient people in their psychological makeup by forcing irrational ideas upon them for very special reactionary political purposes.

JENNINGS: May I say something to that? This is an important distinction that Mr. Ziolkowski made between the phenomenon and the term "myth." However, you can just as well derive another argument from that. If we are concerned with a certain phenomenon, for example, a story which seems especially significant and invites retelling by some mysterious attraction that it has, if we're only talking about that phenomenon, then there is no longer a legitimate basis for making a distinction between old myths and the same phenomenon in modern times. I think it is still the same phenomenon now as it ever was.

WILLSON: I'd like to ask, what happens to old myths when they die?

ZIOLKOWSKI: They become mythology.

WILLSON: They become mythology?

HERMAND: They become literature.

HUDSON: They desacralize.

WILLSON: They demythologize, then?

HUDSON: They lose their surface appearance of sacrality.

WILLSON: Well, I asked the question, because, in regard to Mr. Hermand's statements, what happens when the myths are not there? Does a void ensue? Or what does the rational mind supply? Not that I would endorse the myths that you oppose, because I would not; but I just wonder if there isn't a kind of new creation of myth, in some way? Does modern man create myths that are at all useful to him? Is myth-creation still going on in our society?

HERMAND: Yes, but not by modern man; only special groups with very special purposes engage in this kind of mythmaking in order to dislodge people's minds. I think there's no sense in defending this,

[6] Frank Trippett, "The Hesse Trip," *Look*, February 23, 1971, 53–56.

because it is being defended already by too many people; we have to defend exactly the opposite. We have to defend some kind of rationality, yes, because rationality is weak in the world, and the irrational forces are not. They don't have to be defended; they're just in the majority.

WILLSON: No, we are discussing myth *and* reason; and several times it has been pointed out that there is a connection between myth and reason—that they work together. It has been said that myth and reason—and this is almost paraphrasing Schlegel—work together to attain a unity. No one denies that there are manipulators of myth. But I'm not sure that all mythmakers are manipulators; because myth in a sense springs full-blown from somewhere, not just from one group or one person.

HERMAND: Well, I would say not in the twentieth century, any more; perhaps in archaic societies, but then, our interests are purely historical. We are just interested in the early stages of mankind and how man tried to organize his world view with some kind of mythical concept. What we are really surrounded by—and I think this is not just of historical or academic interest—are the "unmyths" of the twentieth century. They are not primary myths any more; they are second- or third-rate myths.

JENNINGS: I just wanted to mention an example C. G. Jung gives for modern myth: flying saucers. I doubt that there is anyone manipulating this idea in people's minds. I think this just sort of springs up.

HERMAND: On the contrary, I think this is a perfect example of manipulation.

WILLSON: May I just make one statement that has to do with the modern creation of myth—or perhaps "adaptation" is a better word. If we do not create myth today at all, or if the myth that is created today is manipulated myth, then where does myth play a role? Is it possible for myth to play a role in literature today that is a positive, revealing role for the modern mind, for modern man? It struck me recently how many ancient myths are turning up in contemporary German literature. Mr. Middleton, I am sure, knows the series of six poems by Günter Kunert, "Orpheus I–VI." If I had those poems in my pocket I would read you one of them, because in that sequence of six poems, Kunert takes the myth of Orpheus and carries it up to the very present time. It appears that myth can still be applicable. Maybe that's the kind of mythmaking that is going on today.

HERMAND: I think he's not taking over the myth of Orpheus; he's just taking over the literary figure of Orpheus in order to cloak his own personal new concept by combining it with this figure. I don't think it has anything to do with mythmaking. I think rational beings are just incapable of mythmaking.

MIDDLETON: But this is how they are made. Read Dorothy Eggan's essay on "Sam, the Hopi Dreamer."[7] Sam uses the mythology of his people for his dreams, and then he dreams them on. He dreams the mythology onward. In his dreams, for instance, there has been an interesting conversion of a rather amorphous guardian or guide figure from Hopi mythology, who, since Sam dreamed his dreams, has become more concrete and more clearly defined for everyone. So there is this symbiosis, or psychohistorical parallel, as an ethnologically provable fact. I think poets also do this; but they should be pretty careful what they're dreaming.

HUDSON: I'd like to go back to a question Mr. Willson had just a minute ago: whether or not it's possible to invent myths today. Mircea Eliade says it's altogether impossible to invent an entirely new myth. C. G. Jung sees myths as an eruption from the unconscious, the collective unconscious. They come of their own accord. They're virtually inescapable. They assume many disguises and may not be recognized as myths, but they keep coming to us in dreams and in latent meanings, too.

WILLSON: Sometimes the collective unconscious seems to me like the creature from the black lagoon. It's lying in wait to emerge from that oily water and devour us all. But if it's true that mythmaking is no longer possible, and that myth evolves from the collective unconscious, is the collective unconscious gone now?

HUDSON: You get many combinations of mythical elements. You can make rearrangements ad infinitum. I don't buy the collective unconscious.

ZIOLKOWSKI: I don't know with whom I'm agreeing at this point

---

[7] Dorothy Eggan, "The Personal Use of Myth in Dreams: Sam, the Hopi Dreamer," in *Myth: A Symposium*, ed. Thomas A. Sebeok (Bloomington: Indiana University Press, 1965).

any longer. I don't think that myths can be invented intentionally, in one sense; but, at the same time, I do think that modern myths are created constantly, because they are needed. If I accept, as I do, the definition of myth as something associated with ritual, then I look at primitive rites of fertility, or cultic rites in primitive times, or, for a stretch of close to two thousand years, the rites in the Western world of the Christian, and I see myths being created. And if I examine our own society, I look at rituals being performed and think that I detect myths being created behind them also. For instance, it seems to me that a perfectly legitimate, modern, new, noninvented but grown myth is the myth associated with travel by automobile, motorcycle, and so forth: the open highway, "Easy Rider," and so forth. That wasn't invented. It's a legend that probably goes back to the American cowboy and comes up through the automobile and mechanization; but I think that's a perfect example of a legitimate modern myth which grew out of association with some kind of ritual. And I'm sure that there are all kinds of rituals in contemporary technological life that have built up around them forms of behavior which we accept as modern myths.

The second point that I'd like to make—the first was a proclamation of faith—is this: it seems to me that mythmakers, that is, myth-manipulators, whether they're poets or politicians, are successful, like the Ford Motor Company—because the demand is there. People wouldn't make myths, and they wouldn't go to the trouble to manipulate them, if there weren't a deep, basic, inchoate human need for some kind of simplifying explanation for behavior and processes that we call myth. Also, I believe that myth-manipulation is easiest and takes place most successfully when conventional mythic, cultic, ritual beliefs have died out. It's no accident that the most extreme political manipulation has taken place in a highly secularized age in which conventional religious beliefs—church beliefs—have died out or are on their way toward dying out. It's no accident that in our time a basically mythic, ritualistic, religious (if you like) impulse manifests itself among a lot of people in a frenzied search to find religion here or religion there, in the Orient or what have you. I think that this is a very basic human impulse on display here. And, at this point, I'd have to disagree very strongly with Mr. Hermand, who is probably more rational than I am, because I can't conceive (a) that myth today is bad, or not present, and (b) that I would want to live in a society that didn't have myth in some form, but not in one that's run totally by myth.

HERMAND: This brings up the question, of course, Why is there a need for myth? Is it just replacing the old slogan, "Religion ist Opium für das Volk," with "Mythos ist Opium für das Volk"? Why do people tend toward this simplistic view? Don't we now have an obligation to say, All right, you just can't interpret the complexities of modern technocratic societies in this mythical way. There must be something wrong with society when there is a quest for such a simplistic interpretation.

ZIOLKOWSKI: No, when Einstein, toward the end of his life, sought to bring all of his learning, his scientific rational theories, together into what he called a "Unified Field Theory," I think he was mythmaking. At that point he was trying for a grand synthesis that is somehow just a shade beyond what can be reduced to rational explanation. He wanted a grand simplification. Einstein needed that. I think that's an example of a modern myth.

HERMAND: No, I think this was just Einstein's attempt at popularizing a very complex, mathematical matter. I don't think this is mythmaking at all.

SELBY: There are lots of examples. Freudian psychology can be regarded as a very interesting modern myth. If you talk to people outside the pale of academe, even in Western society, they think Freudian psychology is hysterically amusing. People have their own theories and their own myths. The germ theory of disease is another example of modern myth. Nobody in this room understands the germ theory of disease; we just have faith that there are little somethings out there that make you sick. You can't see them; you can't smell them; you can't detect them; they make you sick; and they may kill you. We take that on faith. We have an elaborate ideology of cure, and we have our children inoculated. These are the things we take for granted; they're axiomatic to us, and in that sense they are myth. Myth is something which is with us; it is axiomatic and explanatory, yes. But it also creates problems for which there are no explanations and gives us explanations for which there are no problems. And this dialectic of where myth comes from—it comes from the human mind —is almost a definition of man. He is a classifying animal. Put man on a desert island, he starts classifying. He puts events into categorical structures, and he starts playing with those structures. Thus the origins of man and the origins of myth are coterminous, and the definition of Homo sapiens could be well put in the form: the myth-making animal.

MIDDLETON: Maybe we should open the question period now. I think the people have been very patient.

QUESTIONER: I want to direct a question to Drs. Ziolkowski and Hermand. I'd like to hear both of you try to comment on the relationship between the *Lebenswelt*, the world of the manipulators who stand behind and do what they do with myths, and academe. There have been all kinds of comments about people who start believing their myths too much and then get into trouble. The question was raised: If manipulators are engaged in irrational activity, how do they know what to do? Where do myths reside in this case?

HERMAND: I would not call this myth. I would just call this an appeal to irrational, instinctual forces in men; this is what they try to do.

ZIOLKOWSKI: As I understand it, Mr. Hermand and I have absolutely no disagreement about the semantic meanings that myth, the words "Mythos" and "myth," have assumed in German or in English, or about the history of these forces, and the way that these forces can be manipulated for vulgar purposes. Where I see the disagreement is in Mr. Hermand's unwillingness to accept my feeling that there is, nevertheless, apart from myth in this manipulated sense, also in contemporary society just as in any older, traditional society, still a basic mythic impulse in man that needs to be satisfied and had better be satisfied in a pleasant way or there could be unpleasant consequences. Now that's not really an answer to your questions. That was a clarification of our position, as I understand it.

HERMAND: Yes; and I would not deny that there is a need for this; but I would just turn the question around and ask: Why is there this need? There must be something wrong with society that this need exists or that this very strange irrational need has to be fulfilled by irrational means.

ZIOLKOWSKI: But it's always been there.

HERMAND: Unfortunately, yes.

ZIOLKOWSKI: But at the moment we don't have institutionalized irrationalism . . .

HERMAND: Oh, we have it! We call it politics, now.

ZIOLKOWSKI: But that's the whole problem now. I think that we are accessible to institutionalized irrationalism in political forms just because we don't have institutionalized irrationalism of religious forms, to satisfy those needs that I think are inherent.

HERMAND: All right, they may be satisfied by commercials, advertisements, and so on. There is always this appeal to instinctual gratification. That is how the rationalists manipulate these irrationalities here.

MIDDLETON: If I could maybe interject something at this point: I think there is this phenomenon called "floating irrationality." It may be that we are given this at the moment when we cross the threshold from nature to culture. It may be that the old primary myths were concerned with the problem of floating irrationality. A Marxist, I suppose, would say: No, it is created by economic and social and historical circumstances, and therefore should be rationally eliminated, in due course, using the right means. I think that from much we've said this afternoon and heard before, it would seem that floating irrationality does feed the fundamental salutary structures of true myth, just as much as it is distortable into forms of "unmyth," pseudodoxy, and falsification, and is very much open to becoming the preacher of the manipulators. This is the ambiguous position in which this irrational feature in the human mind seems to stand.

QUESTIONER: I'd like to come back just a second and ask whether the relationship between social forces and the kind of activity that has been talked about could have come to the same resolve in terms of Nazi Germany without the intervention or without the existence of myth at all. In other words, you seemed, Mr. Ziolkowski, to suggest that there was a conjunction of some meanings of the term and social forces that could exist outside of true myth. Perhaps this is something that attention could be turned to. But also, Mr. Hermand has to recognize, for example, the existence of such things in American culture as assassinations, which call up incredible mythical responses among the populace that certainly were not, at least in the sense I understand it, manipulated until after the fact.

HERMAND: Yes, but why do you call this a mythical response? Why isn't this just an irrational response?

QUESTIONER: Well, I think, through some study of political theory, that this is the killing of the king. Even in modern times one of the great gambits in trying to settle World War II was that the Japanese wanted to *certainly* be able not to have the emperor executed. These don't seem to me irrational things at all, but rather, as Mr. Ziolkowski tried to say, they point to a kind of mythical need. I don't see the Japanese people as being irrational for not wanting the emperor to be executed.

HERMAND: But these are of course two very different things. Yes, I think there still was in Japanese society of the thirties—maybe even today—mythical thinking, but not in American society any more. And I think this is a false similarity of the assassinations in America and this mythical killing of the king. These are just two different stages in the historical development of two different societies.

QUESTIONER: I would like you to give me some examples of what you regard as a true myth as opposed to the manipulated or "unmyth."

MIDDLETON: Gilgamesh. The Babylonian creation story. Oedipus.

QUESTIONER: What distinguishes these as truth? What do you mean by true?

MIDDLETON: Well, I don't know what I mean by true, but I do know what I mean by true myth: a story which tells of a series of events which, during the course of the narrative, assume the character of sacred events because they tell of the origination of things; and that can include a hero discovering his own defects. Also a true myth will set up an intricate system of interrelationships between elements, whether those are images or figures or characters. Myth doesn't explain, but gives a deep and perceptive vision of how things occur within the total perspective of human experience.

QUESTIONER: Well, isn't this really simply a distinction between good and bad art?

MIDDLETON: No, no, there's more to it than that, though I couldn't go on. I'm exhausted by that improvised definition.

JENNINGS: I notice that Richard Wagner fits into that pattern. Wagner's *Ring* accounts for the origin of things and has a complex structure. And yet it's a dangerous example of manipulation, in a way.

MIDDLETON: He goes on too long. This is probably a question of structure. The time of which true myths tell is almost out of time. It's the sacred time, it's removed from the succession of moments in which people live and breathe and the rest. I think that the real problem with Wagner is that everything takes a hell of a long time to happen; and this is, in a sense, an attempt to approximate the timelessness of sacred time in terms of extension. It seems to me a complete misunderstanding of what rhythm is about in music, what meter is about, let's say in the Vedic hymns, what motion is about in the movement of the mind.

DUNN: Where would you put James Joyce's *Ulysses*? I mean, do we talk about mythical elements in this, and do we just call it literature, otherwise, and are content with that?

MIDDLETON: Well, I don't know.

DUNN: Is literature just a kind of secondary label that we put underneath?

MIDDLETON: No, I think that *Ulysses* is not just a reactivation, but a re-creation of one of the oldest, profoundest, and, for Joyce, one of the most mystical stories that human beings have ever told one another about themselves. In spite of the magnitude of the fiction Joyce creates, he does squeeze it all into twenty-four hours. That, I think, is quite an important feature here. I'd say that this is one of the most intricate and achieved, realized re-creations of ancient true myth that there is to be read as yet.

DUNN: So there are good re-creations and evil re-creations?

MIDDLETON: There are feeble re-creations and powerful re-creations.

DUNN: But I mean these things that Mr. Hermand talked about yesterday. It seems that there are elements of evil in . . .

MIDDLETON: This is where the retelling counts. Joyce was a supremely reasonable artist, whereas the professors and crackpots and the rest of them, sometimes, well, they're not that. Many of the problems that I've had in reading Hesse have come from my feeling that he sentimentalizes little bits and pieces of mythical material in order to placate some profound creative need in himself he does not realize—that is *Verwirklichung*, re-creation of the original information. What he's providing us with is not a text, but a commentary.

ZIOLKOWSKI: Very often, of course, the origins of myths are lost in preliterate times. We just don't have any documentation. But in some instances we do have documentation, as in the case of Christianity. At some time after the death of Jesus, men started coming together, eating bread and drinking wine together in his memory. And this ritualistic origin of Christianity was celebrated for a number of years before, in the nineties of the first century, the gospel, that is, the myth, was written to explain in considerable detail the meaning of the ritual being celebrated. That is, we have a myth (and I'm using this, here, in the sublime sense), which was created, as it were, to be a description, almost a justification of a ritual that had been celebrated in memory of a presumably historical personage. I think that's an example of genuine myth, and probably similar things could be said about the origin of earlier myths for which we don't have documentation.

Aesthetic structuring, playful use of mythic elements: well, Mr. Seidlin entertained us for an hour and a half showing us how Thomas Mann took that myth of Jesus, but reshaped it playfully to suit his own purposes.[8] This we should call mythological rather than mythic, because it makes a distinction between the primary myth and the secondary myth which is done playfully for purely aesthetic reasons.

Manipulation of myth: We don't need to go to Mr. Hermand's examples from Germany to see how that works; we've got plenty right here. In the eighteenth century the Indian was the noble savage; in the nineteenth century, by manipulation of the myth, he suddenly became the bestial savage who had to be exterminated and driven back to accommodate another myth that had emerged—the myth of the American frontier. American imperialist policy in the western part of the United States, in order to justify its imperialism, had to make a bad Indian out of what a hundred years before had been a very noble savage. That's manipulation of myth in the worst sense. It's not associated with any ritual; it has no holy origin, and yet the

---

[8] He refers to Oskar Seidlin's lecture on "The Lofty Game of Numbers: The Peeperkorn Episode in Thomas Mann's *Der Zauberberg*." See the remarks in the Preface.

strength of this myth is shown by the fact that it survived until the very . . . well, let's say it continues to survive, even though, fortunately, reeducation, rational education is trying to undermine it now. But certainly in the cowboy movies of the thirties and the forties we still had the same myth of the bad Indian in contrast to the noble savage of the eighteenth century. So, I think there are three things to be distinguished: primary myth, aesthetic structuring of mythological elements, and then, finally, manipulation of myth in the most cynical sense.

HUDSON: This manipulation was called forth by current "needs." In French television programs, the Indian is always the noble savage still, today. Always the Indian is right and the white man is wrong.

ZIOLKOWSKI: Well, he's becoming that again in American movies.

MIDDLETON: Yes, the movie *Little Big Man* is somewhat of a modulation of the structure. Lévi-Strauss and others have said that in order to be able to understand a myth you have to be able to read and coordinate all the versions of it. Well, this is a problem for a reasonable man, because when a myth is being made in our own time, we shall not live long enough to see the last petrification of it. This is a depressing thought. More than that I couldn't say. But one can see it happening in this myth of the Indian. Incidentally, the French now are crazy about Tarzan.

Are there any further contributions? Well the aleatory situation has occurred. I hope something has been discovered.

NOTES ON CONTRIBUTORS

HELMUT REHDER, Ashbel Smith Professor in the Department of Germanic Languages at The University of Texas at Austin, is the author of numerous publications largely concerned with the understanding of literature in the light of the general history of ideas, such as his book *Die Philosophie der unendlichen Landschaft* (1932). He is also the author of various textbooks for German. Among his more recent articles are included "Die Anfänge des deutschen Essays" (1966); "Planetenkinder: Some Problems of Character Portrayal in Literature" (1968); and "Reason and Romanticism" (1969).

A. LESLIE WILLSON is presently professor of Germanic Languages at The University of Texas at Austin as well as editor of the journal *Dimension*, which features contemporary German texts along with English translations. He is the author of *A Mythical Image: The Idea of India in German Romanticism* (1964), as well as many articles on Romantic and contemporary writers.

LEE B. JENNINGS is professor of German at the University of Illinois at Chicago Circle. *The Ludicrous Demon: Aspects of the Grotesque in German Post-Romantic Prose* (1963), as well as his many articles, expresses his interest in the psychological symbolism in literature.

JOST HERMAND, Vilas Research Professor at the University of Wisconsin at Madison, has published various books and numerous articles which display his interests in the fields of art history, general history, and literature. Among his many titles are included: *Literaturwissenschaft und Kunstwissenschaft* (1965); *Synthetisches Interpretieren* (1968); and a collection of essays entitled *Von Mainz nach Weimar* (1969).

THEODORE ZIOLKOWSKI, author of books and articles on German and comparative literature ranging from the eighteenth century to the present, is professor of German at Princeton University. His publications include: *Hermann Broch* (1964); *The Novels of Hermann Hesse* (1965); and *Dimensions of the Modern Novel: German Texts and European Contexts* (1969).